Social Media 3.0

It's Easier Than You Think

Social Media 3.0

It's Easier Than You Think

Carol L. Morgan, CAPS, CSP, MIRM

MyHome Press

Social Media 3.0: It's Easier Than You Think
MyHome Press, a Service of the National Association of Home Builders

Elizabeth M. Rich	Director, Book Publishing
Natalie C. Holmes	Book Editor
Forza Design	Cover Design
Pro-Composition, Inc.	Composition
Gasch Printing	Printing

Gerald M. Howard	NAHB Chief Executive Officer
Mark Pursell	NAHB Senior Vice President, Marketing & Sales Group
Lakisha Campbell	NAHB Vice President, Publishing & Affinity Programs

Disclaimer

This publication provides accurate information on the subject matter covered. The publisher is selling it with the understanding that the publisher is not providing legal, accounting, or other professional service. If you need legal advice or other expert assistance, obtain the services of a qualified professional experienced in the subject matter involved. Reference herein to any specific commercial products, process, or service by trade name, trademark, manufacturer, or otherwise does not necessarily constitute or imply its endorsement, recommendation, or favored status by the National Association of Home Builders. The views and opinions of the author expressed in this publication do not necessarily state or reflect those of the National Association of Home Builders, and they shall not be used to advertise or endorse a product.

Printed in the United States of America
16 15 14 13   1 2 3 4 5

Library of Congress Cataloging-in-Publication Data
Morgan, Carol L., 1967-
  Social media 3.0 : it's easier than you think / Carol L. Morgan, CAPS, CSP, MIRM.
pages cm
  Includes bibliographical references and index.
  ISBN 978-0-86718-720-5 (alk. paper)—ISBN 978-0-86718-721-2 1. Internet marketing. 2. Social media. 3. Marketing—Social aspects. I. Title.
  HF5415.1265.M667 2013
  658.8'72—dc23
                    2013009409

For further information, please contact:
National Association of Home Builders
1201 15th Street, NW
Washington, DC 20005-2800
800-223-2665
http://www.myhomepress.com

Contents

About the Author

Carol L. Morgan, MIRM, CAPS, CSP, has more than 20 years of experience as a public relations and social media marketing expert, strategist, and consultant. She is managing partner of mRELEVANCE, LLC, a marketing, communication, and interactive agency with offices in Atlanta and Chicago.

Carol created the nationally ranked and award-winning http://www.AtlantaRealEstateForum.com, an Atlanta real estate blog. She was blogging long before blogging was "cool."

Carol teaches seminars on *social media* to companies and associations nationwide and has spoken at numerous trade shows and conferences including the NAHB International Builders' Show, REtech South, New Media Atlanta, and the Pivotal Galaxy conference. She urges her audience to consider the question, "When you Google your name, do you like what you see?"

Carol holds a BA in business and behavioral science from Oglethorpe University. A member of the Greater Atlanta Home Builders' Association, Carol was honored in 2012 as Council Chair of the Year and in 2008 as Associate of the Year. She is a member of the Georgia Chapter of the Public Relations Society of America and a recipient of PRSA's prestigious George

Goodwin Award. Other honors include the Oglethorpe University 2008 Spirit of Oglethorpe Award, as well as OBIE, Phoenix, APEX, Hermes, and Communicator awards for blogs and client projects.

Carol is a member of the National Association of Real Estate Editors, Public Relations Society of America and Professional Women in Building. She serves on the Board of the Atlanta HBA's Sales and Marketing Council and is the vice chair of NAHB's Professional Women in Building, as well as the Region B trustee.

In her free time, Carol pursues her love of dressage. Read all about her Trakehner stallion Favian *Ps at http: //www.TheBigRedHorse.com (yes, even her horse has a blog). She and her family live at their farm, Thistledown, in Cartersville, Georgia.

Foreword

October 29, 2005, is a day I will never forget. It was the day Blogging Systems, a company I served as marketing director, opened for business on the expo hall floor of the National Association of Realtors annual convention in San Francisco. Our company's sole focus was to bring business blogging to the real estate industry. Our 10' × 10' trade show booth was inundated with agents and brokers who wanted to know how this new form of online communication could help their businesses. I am proud to say that the real estate industry has been a forerunner in the use of this new media.

Since then, social networking sites like Facebook and Twitter have become integral to our cultural landscape. At the same time, consumers have grown more skeptical of advertising and marketing claims that often promise but don't deliver. Instead, consumers trust each other to inform purchasing decisions, including the largest one most people will ever make—buying a home.

Consumers already may have engaged you in their online conversations. It makes perfect sense for home builders, real estate agents, mortgage professionals, and anyone else related to the residential construction industry to communicate with consumers this way. If potential buyers are not talking to or about you, it's time for you to use blogs and social media to kick-start the conversation.

Carol Morgan outlines in a clear, concise, no-nonsense style just how to go about engaging these consumers.

—Paul Chaney, author, *The Digital Handshake*

Abbreviations

CMS	content management system
HARO	help a reporter out
IRL	in real life
ISP	Internet service provider
MT	modified tweet
NAHB	National Association of Home Builders
PPC	pay-per-click
PRT	partial retweet
QR	quick response
ROI	return on investment
RT	retweet
SEM	search engine marketing
SEO	search engine optimization
SERP	search engine results page
SMM	social media marketing
SMO	social media optimization
URL	universal resource locator
USP	unique selling proposition
WIFM	what's in it for me

Preface

I have been immersed in social media since 2005 (or "new media" as it was called way back then). My colleagues and I tested the waters then by posting press releases to a mixture of paid and free online distribution services and pitching stories to real estate agents' blogs. Then one day it occurred to me that I could easily populate a market-focused blog with stories from our clients. With that, Atlanta Real Estate Forum was born into an industry that was skeptical of anything online beyond a basic website.

I have learned invaluable lessons along the way. The intersection of social media and *search engine optimization (SEO)* is powerful for producing results for companies. By using blogs and SEO, our team can typically increase traffic to our clients' websites by at least 20% within six months. Moreover, e-marketing results are easy to measure. My public relations results in the past often were judged on the last big news or feature story my press releases and telephone contacts generated. But now, with social media, *website analytics* provides hard data about important trends like website traffic patterns, and we can tie these to customers' actions.

Eight years after my first experience with social media, Atlanta Real Estate Forum is not only a nationally ranked blog; it's the largest real-estate-focused blog in Atlanta. The site reaches more than 20,000 unique visitors a month and 40% of its traffic comes from outside of Georgia. More important, the blog sends significant traffic each month to home builders who participate by posting stories to the site. But electronic media barely takes a breath before moving on to the next big thing. With the plethora of new social media sites coming and going it can become hard for businesses to keep up, or even know where to start. Success with social media—like any public relations (PR) or marketing strategy—is not about jumping from one "new shiny thing" to another. You build a winning strategy by carefully choosing and targeting audiences. You must use resources wisely. These resources include your time, which can be completely consumed by social media without smart strategies to manage this medium.

Personalized communication and give-and-take, rather than mass media messaging and selling, govern the social media universe. You must give something back, even if it's just honest conversation. Consumers want to know what's in it for them. If they follow you via social media, what will they get in return? Statistics show that consumers follow brands because they expect to get coupons and other special promotions. As a business engaged in social media, you will strategically place "directional signs" on the Internet to help buyers find you. You will also build online relationships with people and companies who influence consumers throughout their buying process. As Paul Chaney says in *The Digital Handshake,*[1] "Social Media is much more than a tool set, it is a mind set as well."

The newest form of *permission-based marketing, social media marketing* (*SMM*), is ever changing and evolving. On the surface, much social networking dialog may seem like idle chatter, but so does cocktail-party conversation or the back-and-forth over 18 holes on the golf course. An important difference between the latter traditional networking activities and social media marketing, however, is that you can use social media also to build your brand, engage consumers, manage your online reputation, engage repeat customers, and make sales—virally and exponentially. To do these things successfully, however, you need the right tools and a comprehensive marketing strategy. Social media can be "easier than you think" when you build on a proper foundation. Make the investment to launch a program with a clear strategy, goals, messaging, and, most important, properly built websites and social sites.

This book will help you create a long-term marketing strategy for building and maintaining an effective social media presence. Happy reading! I hope to connect with you online soon.

http://www.Facebook.com/mRELEVANCE
http://www.Linkedin.com/in/carolmorganflammer
http://Twitter.com/AtlantaPR
http://www.CarolMorgan.net
http://www.mRELEVANCE.com

Acknowledgments

I extend a heartfelt thanks to my family, which continues to look past the craziness of my ideas to see possibilities. Also, to the team members at mRELEVANCE, I owe you a debt of gratitude for the hard work and dedication that transform many of those ideas into reality. To my business partner Mitch Levinson, who was willing to weave his areas of expertise with mine to create great outcomes for our families, our businesses, and our industry: thank you. I also want to give special thanks to my brother, David Morgan, who built my first blog, http://www.AtlantaRealEstateForum.com, taught me about SEO, and opened a world of opportunity. Finally, special thanks to all of my friends and clients who continue to support and inspire me.

The Social Media Mind Set

oday's buyer thinks differently. Perhaps you have heard about *crowd sourcing* and *group think*, but you haven't yet registered what these terms mean for your business. Most consumers are going to ask their *friends* before they buy. This general rule applies to everything from the next book they are going to read, to dinner, to a new car, to a new home. Most consumers—not just the younger ones, or members of *generation Y*—are going to ask before they spend $50 or more. In fact most people, regardless of age, have become comfortable using smartphones, tablets, and texting. They will ask their friends for recommendations of products or service providers on Facebook, Twitter, and other social networking sites. They will also text friends and groups of friends for recommendations. If they want to ask a larger group, read product reviews, or both, they might visit websites like Yelp, Google, and FourSquare. They want to see what buyers have said about your products and their customer service experiences before they buy, but they will expect to see a variety of opinions. Don't feel like all of your reviews must be glowing. In fact, if this is the case, readers are likely to think the reviews were fabricated. It is normal to have a mix of positive, neutral and negative reviews. Some companies have enthusiastic *fans* on the review sites, as well as on their own social sites. Often these raving fans will answer a potential buyer's question before the corporate brand manager even has a chance to review the question, much less respond to it. These companies typically have a great product or service, as well as good customer service and a program to request testimonials and reviews.

Online Researchers

Today's savvy online buyers use the Internet for research. Usually they will start by searching on a major search engine. From there, they jump to corporate websites. After they have narrowed their choices (eliminating sites that are hard to use, display poor quality images, or just don't provide easy access to what they are searching for), they will look to social sites for deals and to gauge how, and how often, a company interacts with fans, and whether those fans really like the company. If your closest competitor is offering coupons and incentives but you aren't, you may lose sales.

In addition, buyers want to try it before they buy it, so not offering a deal can be a deal breaker. My business partner Mitch Levinson calls this "chicken on a stick." When you walk through the food court at the mall, the Asian restaurant will almost always offer you a sample of their cuisine. This sampling technique is often all that is needed to turn "just looking" into a sale. You want to provide your potential customers with this same type of enticement, whether it is a sample, free downloadable white paper, or some other taste of your product or service.

Socially Engaged and Busy

Today's buyer is socially engaged, and you need to be where they are. A significantly larger number of buyers will engage with you on a social site than will complete a "contact us" form on your website, even if they are interested in your product. There are two main reasons for this apparent contradiction. First, a contact form requires personal information, but many buyers don't want to share because they don't want to be added to another email list or get a sales call. Even if they want your product or service, most consumers don't want to be interrupted by sales calls. Second, they are already on the social sites, such as Facebook, to engage with their friends and family. Because these sites are available 24/7, it is much quicker and easier for them to just click to your page and ask a question there than to use Google to find your site, click through search results, and then search and click again to find a contact form.

Therefore, have pages on social sites where consumers already are interacting. If your company has not yet engaged in social media marketing you are missing opportunities for sales. Not being on social sites could cause you to be eliminated early in the consumers' decision-making process.

Furthermore, some buyers are multitaskers. Even if they must provide their phone number, these busy people will, in order to have the convenience of doing other things while they interact with you. Ask buyers how they would prefer to communicate with you; their choices may surprise you. Then follow through accordingly. Interact with them where they want to interact. Be flexible and adapt to what they want.

Overwhelmed with Information

The amount of information available today is overwhelming. My daily junk email and mail are brimming, not to mention the volume of direct messages I get on Twitter and Facebook from companies and individuals trying to sell me something. Although technology is a helpful tool, it is also interruptive. To focus on writing this book I had to turn off email notifications and instant messaging and log out of Mozilla Firefox. However, I still got text messages on my iPhone and alerts from Facebook, Twitter, Foursquare, and myriad other sites. Today's consumer has a short attention span and is completely overloaded with too much information from an ever growing variety of sources. It is more important than ever to apply the "What's In It For Me?" (WIFM) principle to your marketing. The "me" is your potential customer. With so many choices of companies to follow, ask yourself why they should follow yours. Why should a buyer follow or connect with you on your *blog* or other social sites? What are you giving them that none of your competitors are? Whether it is great content, engagement through lively interaction, ongoing contests, or coupons, your social media sites must give something to the consumer in order to get a customer. If they don't see anything in it for them, then your messages are just spam.

Marketing to the Generations

With the economy on the mend and social media gaining an ever greater presence, knowing who to target and how to reach them effectively is a necessary business skill. Currently, three of the largest generations in history *baby boomers, generation X,* and generation Y— simultaneously are influencing markets. Each group has unique wants and needs.

Every generation has been influenced differently by politics, technological advances, cultural shifts, and other factors that impact trust, attitudes about technology, brand loyalty, receptiveness to advertising, and use of social media. However, one key characteristic is true of all of these generations: they are online.

Although in general boomers will respond to more traditional marketing methods such as referrals, open houses, and traditional ads on the web, they are also the fastest growing demographic on social networks and the main purchasers of tablets. Meanwhile, generation X prefers looking at listings and photos online or at blogs that offer expert advice, and generation Y wants to learn more through social media outlets and videos.

Let's use the housing market as one example of an industry where knowing your buyer is key. Generation Y buyers may place a higher emphasis on living close to friends, family, jobs and social centers, and may expect the same amenities they had in college such as a gym, game or billiards room, walking trails, or a pool. Boomers, on the other hand, may expect state-of-the-art kitchens, large walk-in closets, whirlpool bathtubs, fireplaces, and swimming pools. Notice that I've used the word "may." Although generational differences offer clues to your market's preferences, each customer is unique. My point is that as a business owner you must understand your particular customer in order to reach him or her.

Today's most effective businesses maintain their identity but use various marketing strategies so customers with various demographic backgrounds, character traits, and technological proficiencies can relate to their products and services. Buyers don't want to hear a tired sales pitch; they want to know how your products and services meet their needs or satisfy their desires. They want to discover what you have to offer by interacting with you through your Twitter stream, on Pinterest boards, or on Facebook pages. Establish your credibility by demonstrating your expertise. Be transparent—open, truthful, timely, and responsive.

Brand maintenance in the social media realm is a new marketing challenge because everything you post online automatically becomes part of your brand. Your website or blog is at the center of a cohesive marketing plan. But your brand should not be limited to this outlet. You must dedicate time and money to communicating on other social media outlets as well. Existing and potential customers will engage you in conversations using these outlets, and they will notice how, and how quickly, you respond to them. Considering all of the communication options and the age-based characteristics of various markets, pinpointing how best to reach them can be challenging. Using social media to communicate with the various generations can be rewarding. This book explores many ways to reach your target audiences through a robust social media program. When you fully integrate your social networks into your marketing program, you can improve your results exponentially.

Existing Customers

Social media provides an effective way to cultivate your existing customers. We all know that responsibility to your client doesn't end when you make the sale. You need to keep them engaged in a positive way because they are an important source of referrals. Make sure your new home owners are connected with you on all of your social media outlets, and update them with relevant information. For example, provide information about ongoing activities, special events, or new local businesses. Maintain your relationship with them through all buying stages (not just the early stages of information gathering, but also through the assessment and comparison of various similar products, all the way to the purchase and afterwards). Your buyers have the potential to be your biggest advocates for future buyers.

Whomever you are marketing to, make sure you connect with them through their preferred channel and share information that will establish you as a go-to expert—like a trusted friend.

Making Social Media Work for You

Your social media toolbox includes these five elements:

1. Blog (which may be your company website)
2. Facebook
3. Twitter
4. YouTube
5. Other sites including Google+, Pinterest, and strategies such as *online public relations* (*PR*)

To effectively apply these tools, you must first understand three key components of a social media strategy: marketing, optimization, and networking.

SMM is the strategic creation and distribution of content and messages over the Internet via social media, social networking (Linkedin, Facebook), and social bookmarking. SMM encompasses almost every interaction you have online. As with other marketing efforts, you must carefully plan these interactions and deliver them to targeted audiences in the proper context to achieve your goal. When you understand how SMM can increase your company's visibility and website traffic, you can formulate a strategy to maximize its impact.

Social media optimization (*SMO*) is using social media outlets to boost a website's ranking in search engines, such as Google. This powerful tool increases traffic on your website by expanding the number of *keywords* and *referring URLs* search engines will find. For example, searching for "Chicago hot dogs" will return links to websites that are most relevant for these keywords. Social media optimization also refers to the process of modifying each individual social network to rank high in the search engine results.

Social networking is all about engaging others by creating online communities where you interact and converse. Facebook, Linkedin, Twitter, Pinterest, and Google+ are among the social networking sites that allow you to converse and create relationships with friends, fans, and *followers*.

Social Media Marketing Strategy

You would not launch a new company without a business plan, or spend money on traditional advertising without a media plan. Likewise, no social media program should move forward without a blueprint for success. Whether a plan strives to meet one goal or five, it must define what is most important to your social media marketing program. Setting goals allows you to create a sound strategy now and measure *return on investment* (*ROI*) later. Goals must be specific and measurable. Strategies are the steps you will take to meet your goals.

Social Media Marketing Goals

- Increased website traffic
- SMO
- Reputation management
- Engagement through social networking
- Building brand

Increased Website Traffic

Participating in social media and social networking can help you increase the traffic to your main website and your blog. More traffic equals more buyers. Post relevant content online on blogs, social networking sites, and through online public relations, incorporating links to your company's primary website and its blog. This strategy will increase the number of referring URLs for your website and blog. Links provide Internet shoppers with more opportunities to find your business online and click and connect on your website. Think of participating in social networking as weaving a bigger web or placing a sign flipper on just the right street corner to send traffic precisely to where you want it. Appearing in all the places where consumers are already online (like the social networking sites) helps to create a bigger traffic funnel: you capture many users' attention and then focus their search so they eventually land on your website. Leading more traffic to your website can increase the number of lead conversions because effective social media programs tend to garner more qualified leads than other forms of marketing. Principal Management Partners LP demonstrates the effects of a strong SEO and SMO program through increased year-over-year traffic (fig. 2.1).

SEO uses specific techniques to boost your website's ranking in search results for a variety of keywords or phrases. Both on-page (on the website) and off-page (e.g., links, articles, other sites) can achieve positive *organic results*. Organic results appear because of their *relevance* to the term being searched. They are not paid advertisements or *pay-per-click* results. The term *search engine marketing* (*SEM*) refers to marketing via both pay-per-click (PPC) and organic search. If you are purchasing this service, ask what you are actually buying be-

RELEVANCE

Marketing | Communication | Interactive

CTBestApts.com - Traffic Trends for Year 2009-2012 Comparison

	Jan	Feb	Mar	Apr	May	Jun	Jul	Aug	Sep	Oct	Nov	Dec
2009	1,268	1676	2,808	3,221	3,322	3,454	3,414	3,199	2,556	2,517	2,370	2,383
2010	4,023	6,002	8,253	7,290	7,794	6,922	6,685	6,122	5,864	5,497	5,720	5,595
2011	6,842	6,771	8,207	8,663	8,116	8,283	8,916	7,203	5,976	5,777	5,608	5,822
2012	7,378	7,137	6,854	7,742	8,733	8,107	8,362	9,168	6,669	5,798	0	0
% Change	108%	105%	84%	89%	108%	96%	94%	127%	112%	100%	0%	0%

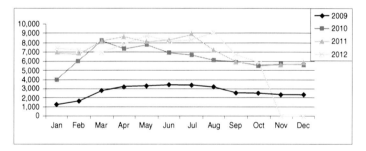

Figure 2.1 **Principal Management Partners LP website traffic**

Tracking website traffic year-over-year allows businesses to gauge increases in traffic. It also identifies seasonal traffic trends that enable strategic marketing and budgeting. (Source: Reprinted with Permission from Principal Management Partners LP, Stamford, Connecticut)

cause often companies selling an SEM service will call it SEO.

SMO (SEO's Cousin)

With 85% of shoppers using Google, Yahoo, Bing, or another search engine to start their online searches, a sound SMO plan should first identify the search terms buyers use to find your company or others like it online. Next, integrate these search terms as keywords into your blog posts, online public relations, and the other content you post as part of your SMM program. When these keywords are used as *anchor text,* search engines will identify your site as relevant for these words and phrases. Think of this relevance as imparting third-party credibility, much like what you get when the local newspaper publishes a story about you.

To maximize returns from using the Internet, you must think like a search engine. This is especially important when blogging and posting to social media sites. One source of information about how Internet shoppers are finding your website currently is your analytics account. You should have an analytics account for both your website and your blog. Many companies use Google Analytics, which provides data for free, but other free and fee-based programs are available. Among these are Yahoo, Webtrends, AWStats, and Urchin.

Anchor text is the underlined word or phrase a user sees and can click to activate a *hyperlink* to another web page. Search engines rank anchor text highly in determining the subject and relevance of a page. Anchor text is sometimes referred to as "linked text."

Reputation Management

After running a number of highly visible reputation management campaigns over the past seven years, I cannot stress enough that you must have a process for handling customer concerns, complaints, and warranty issues. Deleting an unhappy buyer's comments from your Facebook page instead of resolving the issue will only escalate the problem. Therefore, implement a plan for customer service and consider including customer surveys and a loyalty program.

Your reputation is key. Your customers start their search for your product or service online. Make sure you can answer these questions with a positive response: When you Google your name, do you like what you see? More important, when your prospective buyers Google your name, do *they* like what they see?

If you don't like your *search engine results page* (*SERP*), you should implement an SMM campaign ASAP! If you find an unhappy customer's blogs or negative sites on page one of your company's results, you can be certain that potential customers will find them too. To manage your reputation, fill your page-one SERPs with desirable results. A well-built blog and a website with proper SEO should appear consistently among the first four results for your name. You can easily fill up the rest of your page-one results with posts to online PR and social networking sites such as Facebook, Pinterest, Trulia®, Twitter, YouTube, and Flickr,® to name a few favorites.

The specific negative results you have for your name and the strength of those sites will determine how quickly they can be minimized and "moved" to page two. Strong SMO and SEO programs contribute greatly to minimizing negative information.

Of course, remember that today's buyers are seeking honesty. Having both positive and negative reviews on sites like Yelp and Google is OK. But with good products, services, and customer service, your positive reviews should outweigh the negative ones. Part of your plan for reputation management should be to ask happy customers to submit reviews. Although we often forget this step, doing it can be as easy as handing your customer a business card that directs them to a site to post a review of their experience.

The Chicago Wolves demonstrates textbook page one SERP results (fig. 2.2). The sites that browsers see

Figure 2.2 **Chicago Wolves SERP results**

Search your company's name periodically. Identify the search results you want on page one and create a plan to get them. (Source: Reprinted with permission from Chicago Wolves, Chicago, Illinois)

when they Google "Chicago Wolves" include those the ice hockey team created (main website and online store), social networks the company participates in, news sites, ticket sites, Wikipedia, and media coverage of the company. Whether they visit Twitter, YouTube, or Facebook, consumers will find easy ways to access the Chicago Wolves website.

Engagement Through Social Networking

The most popular social networks today are Facebook, Linkedin, Twitter, YouTube, Google+, and Pinterest. But just being on these networks will not build your brand or increase your qualified lead traffic. Unlike push media such as print or radio advertising, social networking is about starting and engaging in conversations, interacting with others, and forming relationships. Customers and potential customers want to understand you and discover your company's personality and culture.

Your social networking should fulfill your brand promise and positioning. If you say you are a customer-service-oriented company, your customers might just test you. Launching pages on Twitter and Facebook tells your customers that you are ready and willing to converse with them, so think twice before jumping on social networking sites merely to blast your latest offer to the masses. Instead, talking with your customers and potential customers creates the top-of-mind awareness that starts to build online brand.

Social media is all about the "me." The main reason consumers friend, fan, or follow brands is to get something. You must provide social networkers with a reason to follow you, such as a coupon or incentive only for the fans who *Like* you on Facebook, or educational content, or a solution to a problem.

Define your audience for each social network. Having thousands of friends, fans, and followers is only effective if they are the right people. Who do you want to reach and what is the right network for each of these target audiences? Consider the following groups:

- Current customers and clients
- Future customers and clients
- *Influencers* (industry professionals, government officials, and cheerleaders who may not be related to your company but who will share your messages)

Building Brand

Companies large and small, including competitors that you may or may not be aware of, are building brand online every minute. Online branding is a comparatively inexpensive marketing alternative ideal for financially challenging times. A first step in branding your company online is ensuring that your company logo and colors are on every website and social site you participate in. They offer a chance to extend your brand beyond your own website and printed materials. Brand and message clarity are essential to avoid confusion among potential customers. Brand goes beyond your logo and promises made in a print ad: it is a lasting impression of your company that can begin with how you and your team answer the phones and sign your email messages, as well as what Internet users find when they search your name online.

Online consumers also learn about you by where they don't find you. When they Google your name, can prospects find you? Do you appear at the top of SERP results when they Google your *unique selling proposition (USP)*? (Yes, USPs apply to online as well as traditional marketing.) Or are they finding your main competitor first? Prospective buyers must be able to locate you where they think you should be, not only in the search engines, but also on social media sites. Can they find and engage with you on Twitter, Facebook, Pinterest, forums, and your blog?

Setting Goals

You can't get where you are going if you don't know where you want to end up. You must create a plan, measure results, and focus on milestones. Whether you want to build brand or manage your reputation, milestones could include launching a blog, optimizing the blog to be among your top five *referral sources,* or getting 200 new Likes on Facebook.

Create Your Strategy

By putting social media tools to work in building SMM and SMO plans, you will attract more online buyers, build a stronger brand, create more loyal customers, and ultimately, increase sales. Although marketing today is different than it was before the Internet, you don't have to reinvent everything. Think about how to adapt what you are doing now to today's marketing environment. You should incorporate SMM into an overall marketing plan just as you do Internet marketing, SEO, events, advertising, and PR. You can use stories, messages, and events to encourage conversations and spontaneity. However, a sound social media strategy ends, rather than begins, with social networking sites. Before you can have SMO, you must first optimize your website and blog.

Integrating social media into your overall marketing mix will streamline your program and make it more effective. Think of your blog or your blog/website as the engine of your program. Your *editorial calendar* will focus on your blog and the blog will pull the entire marketing program together.

Your company's blog or your blog/website links all of your sites together and drives your online image (fig. 2.3). It is the hub of a wheel and the engine of a car. Think of it as your main source of original content for all of your other sites. This makes it your syndication hub and the heart of your online program. It saves time because it refreshes your Twitter and Facebook feeds automatically. Other websites may come and go, but if you have built your program around the piece you own (your blog or website), you will have a strong online presence. Because your blog is the engine of your program, you won't have to worry about what sites are hot today that might become "not" tomorrow. Your blog is your content machine: use it to keep your online presence fresh so as the popularity of third-party sites comes and goes, your blog will remain relevant.

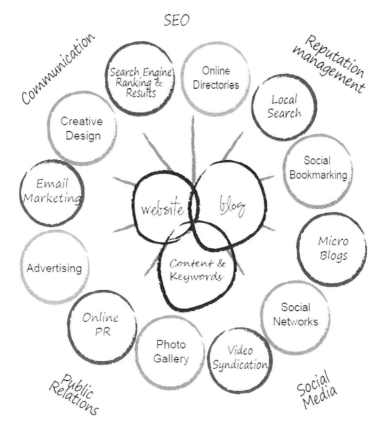

Figure 2.3 The social marketing web

A sound marketing strategy includes social networking, social bookmarking, and photo sharing sites; search engines; syndication (RSS feeds); and email marketing. All roads lead back to your syndication hub, your website, blog, content or messaging, and SEO. (Source: mRELEVANCE, LLC)

3

Websites and Blogs

Your website is central to ensuring all your other online communication is effective. Whether your site is a traditional one or a blog, its elements should build on one another. Review your site to ensure it contains the proper keywords, title *tags*, metadata, and SEO before launching a social media program. The website (or blog) should be

- *sticky* (able to hold users' attention and encourage them to visit multiple pages on the site);
- built with *web 2.0* in mind (interactive so browsers can participate in it and engage with you);
- programmed to capture leads (include multiple ways for Internet shoppers to provide their names and email addresses); and
- easily navigated using mobile devices. In fact, if you have not launched a mobile site, you need to move this task to the top of the list.

Connected and Mobile

Buyers have gone mobile. A June 2012 Motorola Solutions survey of retailers, *The Future of Retail Study*[2] predicts that in the next five years 42% of sales will come from online, mobile, and social commerce sites. Although traditional retailers may not want to believe this, the projection is not outrageous. In fact, according to recent comScore figures,[3] the first quarter of 2012 marked the 10th consecutive quarter of positive year-over-year growth and the sixth successive quarter of double-digit growth for online spending.

Although many retailers understand the need to provide a more engaging in-store experience, a large proportion finds it difficult in practice. To help solve this problem, 51% of retailers are planning to invest in improving customer service. *The Future of Retail Study* offers tips for succeeding as a business in the digital age:

- Complete all transactions via mobile point of sale (POS).
- Offer self-checkout at a terminal or on a shopper's mobile device.
- Route sales through online mobile and commercial sites.
- Send coupons to customers based on their location in a store.

- Provide personalized product details to a shopper's smartphone based on his or her previous behavior.
- Recognize customers who are in the store by using *geofencing* or presence technology. These technologies allow you to determine when customers are physically near your location.

According to a study by Pew Research Center's Project for Excellence in Journalism (PEJ) and The Economist Group, half of all U.S. adults connect to the Internet via a mobile device (tablet or smartphone).[4] Tablet purchases account for a significant portion of the recent boom in mobile growth:

- 22% of U.S. adults own a tablet.
- 3% of adults regularly use a tablet owned by someone else in their home.
- 23% of those who don't have a tablet plan to get one in the next 6 months.
- 44% of U.S. adults have smartphones (an increase from 35% in May 2011).

Website Musts

Mitch Levinson, MIRM, CSP, managing partner of mRELEVANCE, says that an effective website is

- attractive;
- search-engine friendly;
- mobile;
- interactive;
- effective at capturing contact information;
- easy to navigate;
- consistent with the company's brand and capabilities; and
- focused on the target market.[5]

Customers form a positive or negative impression of your company when they land on your website. They might even eliminate you and your products from consideration based on what they see there. Your website must be compelling to get and keep customers. Consider using responsive design for your next website. This is the art of designing a website that adapts to any size screen on which it is displayed. This means that whether your visitor is viewing your site on their smartphone, tablet, laptop or desktop, they will see the content in a user-friendly, readable format that makes sense on their preferred device. Web developers accomplish responsive design by incorporating areas or chunks of content that can be transferred or rearranged depending on the width of the screen on which the site is being viewed.

Instead of building the desktop version of your website first and then your mobile site later, the mobile version of the site is built before the desktop version. The end product delivers a user-friendly experience regardless of the end user's device. Responsive design is different from building completely separate sites with different purposes for each type of device. Although building individual sites can achieve the same result for the end user, the approach is more time consuming.

Responsive design has benefits for users who visit your site, but it also has benefits when it comes to SEO. One way is through usability rankings. Google wants to send visitors to the sites they want to see and that they can easily use, and by having a mobile site that looks the same as your desktop site, but is mobile-device friendly, users will be more likely to spend more time on your site. The other key benefit for SEO is that Google won't see these sites as having duplicate content, which has been a prime target of its Panda update. If you have two sites online with the same content, Google will penalize one of them for being a duplicate. This is based on the assumption that the duplicate site must be promoting content that is not unique.

An effective website will have the following 10 attributes:

1. **Proper SEO.** A website with proper SEO is built in a search-engine-friendly language and contains appropriate keywords and relevant title tags. For ex-

ample, a custom home builder in Des Moines, Iowa, might incorporate the following keywords: Des Moines custom homes, Des Moines custom builder, and custom homes in Des Moines. The main title tag on its home page might read: Name of Building Company—Des Moines Iowa Custom Homes—Luxury Custom Home Builder.

2. **Appropriate keywords.** These relevant words define your business. Also consider the search volume for these words. If people do not know the name of your company, how will they find you? You can use keywords to help them! In the previous example, the descriptors "Des Moines custom homes," "Des Moines custom builder," and "custom homes in Des Moines" can help search engines locate you. If you focus on energy-efficient green homes or specific areas or communities, you should add descriptors appropriate for those areas. We usually start by brainstorming with the entire team of people who work with a company. We develop a long list of words and then narrow it by reviewing search statistics for the quantity and volume of search performed for each word.

3. **Relevant title tags.** These appropriate keywords are search-engine targeted and appear at the top of a website. Each page should have a unique title tag. Too often, companies have home pages titled

"Home Page." Be sure to label each page of your website with relevant keywords. For example, an interior web page might be labeled: Name of Company—About Us—Location or Company Type.

4. **Appealing visuals.** Photos depicting your business must be appealing and professional whether your company is a restaurant, a sports team, a nonprofit, or a child care center. Thoughtfully composed, high quality photos will attract more attention than blurry, cluttered, low-resolution pictures. Consider hiring a professional photographer to shoot these photos or, at the very least, purchase a *DSLR camera* for this purpose. If you are a home builder, for example, think about the home plans you've seen online that are of poor quality, too small, or otherwise difficult to read. Use professional photography and make sure your homes are in pristine condition, including finished landscaping. Note the composition of your photos; anything that detracts from your homes' appearance must be removed, including dumpsters, temporary power poles, temporary yard signage, rock piles, and portable toilets.

5. **Honest representation of company.** Credible information is not only factual but also relevant to the products the company builds. If you build entry-level homes in Atlanta, optimize your site for first-

time buyers and avoid words like "luxury," which might attract a higher-income repeat buyer. The latter buyers will leave your site because your homes are not what they are looking for.

6. **Lead capture.** You must drive website visitors to a contact form so you can capture their information and create a lead. One popular way to do this is with landing pages tailored to specific users. For example, when a potential buyer clicks to your page from Twitter, offer them an incentive on a landing page you have built just for visitors from Twitter. The incentive could be entry into a quarterly drawing for a $25 gift card or some other reward.

7. **Easy navigation.** Your site must be intuitive. Users must be able to find what they are looking for quickly and easily. They should be able to find what they want on their smartphone, tablet, laptop, or desktop computer. Ensure they can locate the information in two to three clicks. This includes directions, hours, and a phone number. And although organized navigation is important, don't let layers of navigation interfere with a consumer's search for information. You can enlist volunteers within and outside of your company to test whether your navigation is intuitive. Ask them to note how many clicks it takes to locate key information about your

company such as products, services, prices, and location.

8. **Stickiness.** A sticky website holds a user's attention, measured by the amount of time spent on it and how deeply a user delves into it. You want visitors to spend three to eight minutes on your site and view multiple pages. You can track progress toward this benchmark over time using Google Analytics or similar programs. Note the web pages where users spend the most time, which landing pages pop up most frequently, and which pages users are on when they exit your site. You can see which pages are the most popular and interesting, and which ones might need fresh content.

9. **Social media interconnectivity.** Make sure your site gives browsers a way to find all of your social media sites including your blog, Facebook page, Linkedin profile, Twitter feed, and other online assets. Often the information and connections buyers make through social media convert them from just online visitors into buyers.

10. **Call to action.** The website must guide the user to interact with you. It should seek user contact information and provide various options for a user to contact you. Use the website to encourage visitors to call the telephone number on your site, drive to

your sales center, or contact you using an online contact form. Provide multiple ways for people to contact you by including all of your community phone numbers on the site, contact forms for each community, and a form users can complete to start receiving your newsletter.

The Blog as a Website

Rejuvenate, an AVEDA Concept Spa & Salon, uses a blog for its main website (fig. 3.1). Savvy web development teams are building sites using *content management systems* (*CMS*) created specifically for blogging. If you are building a new website and want to include a blog, consider building the entire website on a blog platform, such as WordPress. Like printed brochures, most websites are designed to be updated less frequently than a blog. However, content management software with a user interface, such as WordPress, facilitates frequent updates. In addition to blogging, non-technical users can learn to update other areas of the site using content management software.

Why Blog?

A properly built blog is the engine that drives a successful social media program. When you combine great writ-

Figure 3.1 Rejuvenate's blog/website home page

Your custom blog can look just like a website. In fact, it can be your website!
(Source: Reprinted with permission from Damaris Waters, Cartersville, Georgia.)

ing, phenomenal images, and SMO in a blog, you have a formula for success. Companies should blog for three primary reasons: (1) to better control the company's image and reputation, (2) to increase the SEO of the main website (through SMO), and (3) to create a platform to engage and interact with buyers. Establish the objectives for your blog, such as

- attracting search engines;
- enticing readers to visit the company's main website;
- encouraging direct company contact and interaction; and
- building participation in an online or off-line event or activity.

What's in a Blog?

The word blog is a contraction of two words, web and log. The first blogs were like online diaries or journals. Today the blog is a website focused on a particular subject or area of expertise. Posts are displayed in reverse chronological order: the most recent post will display at the top of the page.

In addition to engaging online shoppers in an informal conversation, a well-built blog can expand the

SEO of the main website by increasing the number of keywords and referring URLs—two objectives of social media optimization.

Blogging Nets ROI

Industry-focused blogs such as Green Built Blog (http://www.GreenBuiltBlog.com) demonstrate the value of blogs (fig. 3.2). They provide spaces for multiple companies to attract potential buyers through the search engines. Sites like this help builders expand their keyword reach through SMO. With hundreds of keywords indexed monthly by Google, this site is a top referral source for many home builders, developers, and their communities.

The blog connects buyers to a company website through search. Although most websites can be optimized for only 5 to 10 keywords, a blog can attract search engines with hundreds or even thousands of keywords. By expanding keywords and anchor text, blogging can increase the traffic to a website exponentially. By design, when a new post is written and published, a new page is created on the blog. Fresh content keeps attracting the search engines and providing new pages to index and your website's relevance vis-à-vis keywords in the posts continually increases.

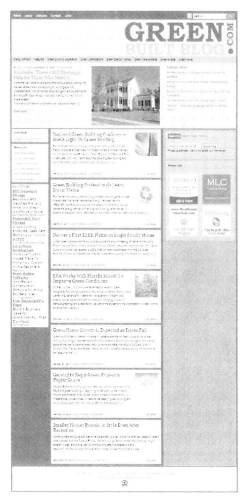

Figure 3.2 **Green Built Blog**

A highly optimized new homes news blog featuring green building news, Green Built Blog attracts about 45% of its traffic from consumers searching keywords in the search engines. (Source: mRELEVANCE)

Blogging Schedule

When establishing your schedule for blog posting, consider that most people prefer to read blogs in the morning. Peak blog reading occurs at around 10 a.m. while people are at work. In fact, if you look at your website traffic you will see that the majority of Internet browsing occurs Monday through Friday when consumers are at work.

Your blog can grow by as many as eight pages per month (if you add eight posts a month), whereas most websites don't add new pages monthly, even if the sites are updated frequently. This is one of the main reasons that a well-built blog will perform well with the search engines over time.

Of all the tools, sites, and social media strategies, a blog is the likeliest to net ROI and show almost instant success. A well-built optimized blog will become a top referral source for the company website. Your blog will probably be among your top five website referral sources within a few weeks of launching it.

"The State of Inbound Marketing," (HubSpot), found that businesses know their blogs are valuable. Some 62% of companies have a corporate blog and 81% of businesses rated their company blog as useful, critical, or important. A full 25% rated the corporate blog as a critical component of their business.[6]

The study also found that blogs were a major source of leads, followed by social media and organic SEO. Moreover, blog posting frequency correlates with the number of leads that corporate blogs are able to convert to customers; 57% of companies have gained a customer as a result of blogging.

Traton Homes Attracts Traffic

Traton Homes embraced social media with the launch of http://www.TratonHomesBlog.com (fig. 3.3). This Marietta, Georgia, builder of townhomes and single family homes in the Atlanta metro area has increased keywords and referring URLs for the company's main website by creating a blog. Within 30 days of launch, the blog became one of the top 10 referral sources for the company's main website.

The blog offers prospective home buyers the opportunity to connect with the company and learn more about Traton's homes, communities, and the company. More than 50% of traffic to the company's blog was from search engines and free referral sources. More than 70% of traffic to the blog was new. If you Google "Traton Homes," page one search results will include the com-

Figure 3.3 **Traton Homes blog**

The Traton Homes blog is a top referral source for the Traton Homes website.
(Source: Reprinted with permission from Traton Homes, Marietta, Georgia.)

pany's blog, YouTube, Twitter, Facebook, and Linkedin
pages.

The Traton Homes blog keeps home buyers abreast
of community news, local events, and special promotions. It also features videos of specific communities and

the home page always features a community. Home shoppers can access the builder's top-selling communities directly from the blog.

Creating Your Blog: Getting Started with WordPress

Follow these 12 steps to create a self-hosted WordPress blog and measure its effectiveness:

1. **Name your blog.** http://www.NameofCompanyBlog.com is a popular choice. Another option many companies choose is http://www.NameofCompanyNews.com. You can purchase your domain name from a domain reseller like http://www.GoDaddy.com, http://www.Register.com, or http://www.Domain.com.

2. **Determine hosting for your blog.** Your blog may be hosted on the same server as your main website, but often you will need to explore other options. Some low-cost options include http://www.BlueHost.com and http://www.HostGator.com, but consider instead hosting your site at a premium hosting location. This will provide you with more control so that no known *spammers* are hosted with you. You will also be able to get a unique ISP address for your site.

Run Software Updates

Blog software is open source and frequently updated. To maintain a blog's functionality, to ensure *plug-ins* work, and to reduce security risks, blog software must be updated as new versions are released. Depending on the complexity of your WordPress site, updating your software can be as easy as clicking a link.

3. **Choose a *theme* and categories.** Many free or inexpensive templates and themes are available for blogs, or a web developer can create a custom theme for you. You can choose from a number of free themes at WordPress.org.[7]

4. **Determine keywords.** What words will customers use to find you? Make sure you have a plan for using them in your blog. For example, if you build energy efficient homes, you will want to include "energy efficient homes" in your list of keywords along with "Name of City real estate," "_____ sized lots in Name of City," and other variations.

5. **Go to http://www.wordpress.org to download blogging software to your URL.** You will want to research available themes and plug-ins and download those as well. Most people will need to hire a web developer to complete this step.

6. **Create an editorial calendar.** Set a schedule for posting on your blog. You should publish eight entries per month. Vary the days you post to keep the search engines guessing about when you will post. Internet traffic is highest during the week, so post Monday through Friday.

7. **Create a blog policy.** It should address how comments will be moderated. Refer to the next section or Google "blog policy" for other examples.

8. **Assemble your blogging team.** This is not necessarily your marketing team. Which staff members love to write or compose video? Include them! We work with a number of blogging teams that incorporate members of the sales team, marketing representatives, and the president or CEO of the company.

9. **Launch your site.** Change the *A record* or name servers in your DNS (domain name server) account to point to the new blog and make it live. It can take up to 24 hours to propagate through the Internet.

10. **Install Google Analytics.** You can find a step-by-step guide for adding this *tracking software* to your blog at Google http://www.google.com/support/analytics/bin/answer.py?hl=en&answer=66983.

11. **Promote your blog.** Burn the *real simple syndication* (*RSS*) feed, and connect the blog to Twitter, Facebook, and other social networking sites. Reg-

ister the blog on blog catalogs such as Technorati, Blog Catalog, and Best of the Web. Make sure to promote your blog from your social sites, your website, and in your email signature.

12. **Measure results.** Use Google Analytics to track key performance indicators such as number of visitors, time on site, and most popular content. The new social tracking option from Google allows you to track visitors on your site who come from the social networks. It shows how many visitors are coming from your social sites and which sites refer the most traffic. Note where they go once they are on your website; you can use this intelligence to give social-media-minded buyers more of what interests them.

Establish a Blog Policy

It is important to have a blog policy on your site that meets Federal Trade Commission (FTC) guidelines and lets your readers know how content and comments are handled. Advertisements that include endorsements and testimonials must disclose any connection or relationship between the advertiser and the endorser.

This pertains to blogs just as it does to "word-of-mouth" marketing. Specifically, if a blogger receives cash or an in-kind payment to review a product, and then endorses it, the FTC considers this relevant to the endorsement and the quid pro quo must be disclosed.[8]

Sample Policy

The following policy statement governs Atlanta Real Estate Forum's blog:

Disclosures

In order to comply with recent FTC Rulings, Atlanta Real Estate Forum discloses the following: This blog was launched as an online extension of public relations coverage for mRELEVANCE's clients. The site accepts advertisements and sponsored posts. Atlanta Real Estate Forum is proud to publish news 365 days a year. Currently more than 100 contributors from the Atlanta real estate industry create stories for the site. The blog also covers industry news via our team of talented reporters. Nonprofit news is covered as a community service. Oh, and yes, those are Google ads on the left side of the site.

Rules of Engagement

By posting to Atlanta Real Estate Forum you agree that you are responsible for the content you contribute, link to, or otherwise upload. All posts and comments must be related to the subject matter covered by this site (real estate). You agree not to post anything threatening, libelous, defamatory, obscene, inflammatory, illegal or pornographic, or anything that infringes upon the copyright, trademark, publicity rights or other rights of a third party.

We welcome comments, but please understand that all comments are moderated and reviewed for relevance to site topics. Comments and posts will be published at the sole discretion of mRELEVANCE. Your valid email address must be used when you post or comment. It will not be published, but may be used to confirm your identity or contact you with questions.

Atlanta Real Estate Forum strives for accuracy; however, with the large number of contributors on the site we assume no liability for errors or omissions. You transfer rights to Atlanta Real Estate Forum for any original content you provide.

By using our site, you agree to our policies and rules of engagement.

All rights reserved. Reproduction of material from any pages on Atlanta Real Estate Forum without permission from mRELEVANCE, LLC is strictly prohibited.

Free Blogging Options

Free blogging options include the complimentary version of WordPress (http://www.wordpress.com), Blogger (http://www.blogger.com), Tumblr (http://

www.tumblr.com), or Real Estate Sites Hub (http://
www.RealEstateSitesHub.com).

You also can blog on real estate industry sites such
as ActiveRain, Trulia, RealtyJoin, or Realtor.com, and on
local blogs where you can share your expertise as a guest
blogger or a regular contributor. Consider Realtor,
newspaper, and new home sites such as Atlanta Real Estate Forum, Luxury Real Estate Forum, Green Built
Blog, and New Homes Section.

Form Follows Function

Blog designs vary, as the examples in this book illustrate.
Free templates have basic designs, but you can create
and customize more elaborate blogs. Before choosing
your design, consider how it will function in the future.
In addition to current posts and an archive of previous
posts, the blog should include

* "About" and "contact" pages, like these:
  http://www.atlantarealestateforum.com/about/
  http://www.atlantarealestateforum.com/contact/
* A disclaimer page, like this:
  http://www.highlandhomes.org/news/
  disclaimer-highland-homes/

You also may want to include banner advertisements, featured news, or both. Some themes, such as

those on http://www.chicagolandrealestateforum.com and http://www.luxuryrealestateforum.com, include a section with featured news or featured articles. This content appears at the top of the page, right under the *masthead*. Featured news does not change as frequently as the regular blog posts on these sites.

If you are considering including banner advertisements on your site, you will need to know how many unique visitors your site gets in a day, a month, and a year, and how many impressions an ad will get. The amount you can charge for ads typically depends on how much traffic your site receives. You can charge a flat fee per month, per click, or per engagement. Cost per engagement is still a relatively new way to charge for advertising. This method of determining return on investment can measure likes, mouse-overs, shares, downloads and responses, for examples. You also need to determine where to place ads. They can be banner ads above the masthead or they can be placed lower on the right or left side of the page. A builder might accept advertising for a building product or a restaurant near one of its popular communities. An HBA can accept ads from builders too. Springfield HBA (http://www.springfieldhba.com) has a number of advertisers featured on its blog/website including builders, inspection companies, design centers, and appliance resources.

Widgets, Plug-ins, and Other Gadgets

Often the words *widget* and plug-in are used almost interchangeably. They both refer to small *applications* of code you can install in a blog or a website after it is built, like aftermarket car accessories. Typically these bits of code can't function alone but they can enhance a larger software application like the one your blog uses. Some of these widgets, plug-ins, and other gadgets add functionality and interactivity to help users engage with your site. Others are management tools for you. Some of the most popular ones used with WordPress are completely invisible to users. mRELEVANCE uses these:

- **All in One SEO Pack.** This is favorite tried-and-true plug-in helps perform SEO on each blog post. Yoast is another good SEO plugin.
- **Akismet.** This is the ultimate spam catcher. It will check comments on your blog and sort them into a spam folder for you to review. It reduces the time commitment to moderate your blog. Cookies for Comments is another spam catcher.
- **NextGEN Gallery.** This is an image gallery plug-in with an optional slideshow. Your visitors can view your plans, finished homes, and communities.

- **BuddyPress.** This plug-in allows you to operate your blog as a social networking site. Users can create profiles, post messages, make connections and interact between groups. RealtyJoin uses it.
- **WP-Polls.** With WP-Polls you can easily incorporate a poll into a post or a page on your blog.
- **Facebook Like.** This plug-in makes it easy for your readers to Like your content and share it with their friends.
- **Facebook Like Box Widget.** This plug-in adds an entire Facebook Like box to your blog so readers can Like your Facebook page.
- **Facebook for WordPress.** This is the official Facebook plug-in for WordPress and WordPress.com. The goal of this plugin is to make WordPress more social. It is even mobile ready.
- **Sociable.** This plug-in allows your readers to share the posts they like with their friends. When you configure it, you can choose from among hundreds of sites where users can share your content, including Twitter, Facebook, Digg, Delicious, Sphinn, Mixx, and many more. You can also allow readers to email your posts or print PDFs of them. Social Media Widget is another favorite for social sharing.

You can also use plug-ins to add a calendar, your Twitter feed, a countdown timer for a big event, and many more features. You install and activate plug-ins from the WordPress dashboard. Visit WordPress (http://www.wordpress.org/extend/plugins/) to browse thousands of plug-ins. If you have ever thought, "I wish my blog could . . ." it probably can. Don't get carried away with the bling; installing too many gadgets will distract users and make your blog slow to load and respond. You should load and activate basic plug-ins to control spam comments, generate site maps, and enhance SEO. Focus on your blog's mission and functionality.

The Magic of Keywords

Before you write your first blog post, schedule a meeting with the interactive agency, consultant(s), or in-house staff member(s) responsible for your website's SEO. As a group, review your website's analytics, noting the keywords the site already attracts. What are the obvious missing keywords? As you plan your keyword strategy for your blog, identify the words and phrases that your main site is not successfully attracting and ensure that your blog includes them. Blogs successfully attract *long-tail keywords*—typically product-specific phrases of three to five words. For instance, rather than searching for the word "car," a buyer might search for "1960 restored red Mercedes Benz."

Including the right keywords has become even more important with the onslaught of Google updates in recent years. Google Caffeine[9] and Google Instant were the beginning of the important updates that impact social media. Released in June 2010, Google Caffeine provides 50% fresher results than previous Google indexes because it refreshes search results continuously. New optimized blog posts appear in search results more quickly than they used to.

In addition to including long-tail keyword phrases in your blogs, also home in on short keywords to bring up your company in the search results as the words are typed. Google's "Instant" feature is a search enhancement that provides results as a user types. For example, if he or she is searching for Atlanta Real Estate, by the time the user types "atl," Google is offering results.

Google's 2012 updates—Panda and Penguin— make you wonder what is going on at the zoo. The Penguin update *algorithm,* released in 2012, still has the most kinks to work out. The update was initially designed to penalize sites that spam Google, but Google officials have said the update is merely an adjustment to reduce this spamming. Specifically, certain linking activities such as using specific keywords to link to your site from third-party sites or to link deeper within your site that worked in the past seem to no longer be effective and in many cases can be detrimental. This type of linking can still be performed effectively, but you must have a plan for doing the job strategically to avoid repetitive linking.

The Panda update, released in 2011, was created to penalize websites with poor quality content in the search results. Since then, each update has produced changes in the search results, but each one seems to have a less dramatic effect.

What does all of this mean for your company? Because SEO tools and tactics are ever changing, you must change how you handle SEO with each new search engine update. To ensure your company stays on top of search results, you will need to either dedicate a lot of time to SEO activities or hire an agency that specializes in SEO on an ongoing basis. If you have noticed your site slipping off page one for certain keywords, you could be overly or improperly optimized. Make sure to hire a company experienced with SEO to analyze your rankings and help you create a plan that can coexist with all of the Google animals.

Blog Content Ideas

Stumped about what to write? Here are 10 ideas for blog posts that would work for a home building company, for example. Think about your company's products and blog about them.

1. Discuss the latest ideas for kitchen organization and demonstrate these features in a companion video.

2. Introduce your new community with a post on the top 5 reasons why home buyers want to live there, including its location, amenities, quality, and value.

3. Explain your 10-point quality inspection program and videotape a mock walk-through with your construction superintendent.

4. Educate your buyers on available loan products.

5. Show and explain available options for carpet, cabinetry, tile, and lighting, using photos or video.

6. Invite readers to an upcoming home show or Parade of Homes you participate in. Discuss your homes and communities and link to the show or the Parade's main website with information on all the homes.

7. Videotape a testimonial from a happy home owner. This could be a remodeling customer talking about her new kitchen (with before and after images), a new custom home owner, or a family who lives in one of your planned communities. Include a photo or video testimonial to make it more real.

8. Discuss the energy-saving features you incorporate into your homes. Explain the details about what makes new homes more energy efficient than used homes.

9. Introduce your new colors, styles, and features for spring, summer, fall, or the new year. This works for suppliers introducing new products, builders with new plans, and designers featuring the latest trends.

10. Showcase your charity work, whether it is donating countertops to a community group home or providing a crew to finish a HomeAid house. Tell your readers how they can participate.

What Readers Want

A good blog post is written both for the consumer and for the search engines. It contains unique content, visuals (photos and video), audio, keywords, anchor text, and links. Blog posts don't have to be long; they can be 250–350 words. Shorter posts might not have enough content to capture the search engines. Longer ones might discourage distracted readers without a lot of time for reading or viewing. Video posts include a video embedded from a site such as Vimeo or YouTube and a brief written description of the video. The short (150 words or so) video post will help search engines properly index the video. All posts should be conversational and interesting. Ask readers questions to start conversations. Write about topics that ignite your passions.

The most effective posts will provide the information most buyers are seeking, so describe your community's location, homes, and amenities. Readers also may want to know how to obtain financing or receive tax and energy credits.

Top 3 lists, Top 5 lists, and bulleted information attract attention. It is always a good idea to break up large blocks of text into steps or other lists using bullets. This makes it easier for readers to absorb the information and understand what action to take. Don't forget to include a call to action in each post. For example, place a question at the end to encourage further interaction. There are some great examples of calls to action on the daily SEO Blog on SEOmoz.[10] To encourage reader engagement, consider the following:

- What action do you want readers to take? (Think comments, social shares, clicks, subscribes, and, most important, purchases!)
- How have you inspired them to take action in the past?
- How does your content contribute to successful interactions? (Is your content provocative, visionary, relevant, current, timely?)

Following are four examples of effective blog posts. Although each builder took a different approach, all four are equally engaging because they captivated readers and got them to act. Let's dig into what makes each of these a good post.

S&A Homes: Easy E-Incentive

S&A homes announced an e-incentive for Realtors on its blog (fig. 3.4).[11] The post encouraged Realtors to Like the new S&A Homes Facebook page. Each new real estate agent who liked the page and wrote a comment about working with S&A Homes received a $10 Sheetz gift card for gas. The post included three simple steps for agents to complete to get the gas card. Providing an incentive to a target audience to encourage them to do something is also a great way to build a following among the groups you want to follow you, like Realtors.

Gerstad Builders: Educating Buyers

In addition to posting on its own news blog, McHenry County home builder Gerstad Builders frequently contributes content to http://www.ChicagolandRealEstate Forum.com (fig. 3.5). The posts educate potential home buyers and drive traffic to the builder's website. For example, Gerstad contributed "4 Tips to Improve Your Credit Score."[12] The post listed the tips, quoted industry expert Ilyce Glink, and linked to her blog at Think Glink for additional information. Using expert sources adds

Figure 3.4 **S&A Homes E-centive**

S&A Homes incentivized Realtors to Like its Facebook page. (Source: Reprinted with permission from S&A Homes, State College, Pennsylvania)

Figure 3.5 Chicagoland Real Estate Forum blog post

Gerstad Builders uses its blog to educate home buyers and help make the buying process easier. (Source: Reprinted with permission from mRELEVANCE, LLC.)

credibility to your blog posts, so interview and quote experts, and link to their sites. They may link to your post, *tweet* about it, or post it on Facebook.

Boone Homes: What's Not to Like?

You can use a literary device, such as irony, to engage readers on your blog and educate them about your USP. Chris Parks with Boone Homes demonstrates this with a tongue-in-cheek post titled, "The $6^{1}/_{2}$ Best Reasons Not to Build a Boone Home"[13] (fig. 3.6). For every reason he gives not to buy a Boone Home, he adds a positive counterpoint telling readers why buying one is a good idea. Experiment to find a writing style you are comfortable with. Use titles that will spark readers' curiosity.

Airing the Dirty Laundry

To elicit interaction, ask readers a question at the end of a post, or highlight an unusual or often-overlooked home feature. In the post, "Laundry—the Easy Way,"[14] Laura Spencer of Boone Homes writes about laundry room organization (fig. 3.7). Laura engages blog readers by discussing her personal experience with getting a 12-year-old to put her laundry where it belongs. Then she shows how having an organized laundry room, like

Figure 3.6 Boone Homes blog post example 1

Capture blog readers' attention with interesting headlines. (Source: Reprinted with permission from Boone Homes, Richmond, Virginia)

those Boone Homes builds, makes laundry an easier task.

Multiple readers responded to the post thanking Laura for writing it and commenting on how small their own laundry rooms are. Do you sense there were move-up buyers reading?

Use personal experiences readers can relate to and they will read your blog and, possibly, buy a product from you.

Use your blog to establish your expertise, whether it's green building, homes for first-time buyers, remodeling for aging in place, energy efficiency, interior design, mortgages, credit repair, or landscaping. Choose topics you enjoy talking about and your enthusiasm will show.

Still have writer's block? Read the paper; read other local blogs; follow top real estate agents on Trulia, ActiveRain, or Realtor.com for inspiration.

Blogging with Impact

After you write your first blog post, edit it (or better yet, ask another person to do so), and tweak it for the search engines. Make sure it includes the keywords the search engines should associate with the post. For example, if your blog post is about best plants for winter gardening, your keyword phrases might include "winter gardening," "planting during winter," or "flowers that grow in

Figure 3.7 **Boone Homes blog post example 2**

Give readers something to relate to in your blog posts. Boone Homes does just that by talking about laundry and teenagers. (Source: Reprinted with permission from Boone Homes, Richmond, Va.)

winter." Include two or three relevant keywords or keyword phrases in each blog post, but don't randomly add keywords just to try to boost your search results; your blog needs to be readable. *Stuffing* keywords into a post is content spamming: it will annoy your readers and may actually harm your search engine results. In fact, Google launched updates recently to combat keyword stuffing and keyword spamming.

Next, add links from your post to other sites. Links give readers the opportunity to discover additional information. For example, when a post references a company or organization, hyperlink its name to its website. Also consider incorporating your company's keywords as anchor text. For example, if you referenced Orange County townhomes in a post, you would link the words "Orange County townhomes" to the community page on your website that discusses the townhomes. Each blog post should have one to three links to other sites. At least one of these should go to a page on your main website, but rather than always linking to your home page, regularly link to other pages within the site. Consider linking to previous posts to your blog as well. If your post references a topic or event discussed in a previous post, link to that post.

Keep It Fresh

More than 95% of blogs are abandoned.[15] Launching a blog is a major commitment. You must be dedicated and willing to post consistently. There is nothing worse than stale content. When a site visitor clicks on an events page only to find last year's events, they are frustrated and your brand is tarnished. You don't want to eat stale cereal, and neither do your readers. Determine how often you can post; create an editorial calendar; and stick to it.

If the main goal of your blog is SMO, plan to post two times per week. By varying the day and time of each post you will keep the search engines coming back to your site more often in search of fresh content. This is generally a good dose of content for readers, too—just enough to keep them coming back, but not enough to overwhelm them.

Manage the Blog

One individual should manage the blog, although various authors can write or contribute content to it. The blog manager or moderator could be an employee or whoever handles your marketing or PR. The blog manager will

- oversee the blog schedule;
- review the editorial content;
- ensure that writers post content regularly; and
- moderate the blog.

The moderator will ensure posts contain keywords, anchor text, and links; monitor and respond to comments; and forward comments that require a response to the appropriate individual.

Because they offer a variety of perspectives and voices, some of the most interesting blogs have multiple authors. However, readers expect transparency, so tell them who is blogging on your corporate site. Consider having the president, marketing director, members of the sales team, and others contribute. Create an individual profile for each blogger so a writer can build his or her own personal brand and voice. Invite guest bloggers to post on your site.

Budget Time

Budget 20 hours a month for eight posts. Each blog post will probably take at least an hour to write, depending on how much research the topic requires and whether you will have to search for a visual, such as a photo, illustration, or video. Plan another 30 minutes for your blog manager to moderate each post.

Follow Copyright Law

Just because content is posted online does not mean you can copy and paste it to your own blog. Like other published works, online content is covered by copyright law. Cutting and pasting stories from your daily newspaper, business journal, favorite social media, real estate blog, or any other website violates the law. You can reference, quote from, or paraphrase material that you see or read online by following "fair use" guidelines that go hand in hand with copyright law. However, be cautious in doing so, especially when you are using the material for commercial purposes. Acknowledging the source of the copyrighted material does not substitute for obtaining permission. No specific number of words, lines, or notes may legally be taken without permission.[16] To protect yourself, get written permission if you want to republish material. For more information on fair use, visit the U.S. Copyright office online at http://www.copyright.gov.

Don't Plagiarize

Remember what you learned in elementary school: don't plagiarize. You may reference an article with proper credit to the original source and link to it, but don't cut and paste text or images onto your site without written permission from the original author and/or the publisher.

> Use your editorial calendar. Plan your posts at least a
> month before they are scheduled to run.

In addition, be aware that search engines like Google work to index pages with original content, and they will index the first or the most relevant post when there is identical content. So, even if you get permission to use information from another site, it is not a good SEO strategy. In fact, a search engine may remove from its index a site with duplicate content.[17] Then the site no longer will appear in search results.

Photos

Copyrights apply to photos and illustrations as well as written work. Penalties can be as high as $20,000 per image, not to mention court costs. If you want to use others' content, first verify that it is available for you to use under the *Creative Commons* license. This copyright license permits distribution of others' content within specific guidelines.

If you find valuable content that you want to reference, mention it (rather than copying and pasting it) and be sure to credit the original source, which may be different from the website where you found the material. You can discuss why you like the content, paraphrasing one or two main points, and its relevance for your readers. Then write your own conclusion, in your own words, to your post.

Copyright discussions have gotten heated with recent changes made on the popular photo sharing site, Pinterest. Pinterest put the burden of copyright proof back with the person posting the photos. In other words, they asked posters to only post photos that they own the copyright to or have permission to use. Pinterest users rebelled against this policy and Pinterest changed its terms again to be a bit more lenient. You can view its policy at http://pinterest.com/about/copyright/.

Promote Your Blog

If you build it, they will come—but only in the movies. When it comes to your blog, you must tirelessly promote it to get people to come to it. Invite readers to sign up for your email or RSS feed or read your blog through their preferred feed. This is like subscribing to a newspaper or newsletter, but readers get to choose how their content is delivered.

Netweave all of your Internet marketing. This means including a link to your blog on your website, in your email signature, on your banner ads, in your email marketing, on your social networking sites, and anywhere else you can find a place to include a link or an icon. Format your blog to tweet your latest post and use Networked Blogs or RSS Graffiti (*see* Resources) to connect your blog to your Facebook fan page.

Commenting on other people's related blogs is a great way to attract visitors to your blog. For example, if you are a green builder, comment on various green blogs. Just ensure that your comments are relevant, not spam.

Finally, register your blog with the blog directories Technorati and Blog Catalog.

S&A homes (http://www.SAHomesBlog.com) does an excellent job of netweaving. Its blog's home page prominently displays links to the company's social media sites and to a form users can complete to subscribe to the blog. The blog features a video from the builder's YouTube channel on the home page (fig. 3.8). *Sociable icons* placed at the bottom of each blog post encourage readers to share their favorite content.

Track Users

To gauge whether your blog is meeting expectations for unique visitors, how much time they spend on the site, and the number of pages they visit, you need tracking software. Most blogging platforms offer at least a rudimentary tool for this. For a self-hosted WordPress blog, track performance with Google Analytics.

Figure 3.8 **S&A Homes blog**

S&A Homes prominently features video on the home page of its blog. (Source: Reprinted with permission from S&A Homes, State College, Pennsylvania)

Review tracking data monthly, noting month-over-month and year-over-year trends. Besides measuring your blog's success; you will be able to see cyclical patterns in your online traffic. It may increase or decrease seasonally depending on your business. Pay attention to the following data:

- **Number of unique visitors to your blog.** What is the proportion of returning visitors to new visitors?
- **Average time each visitor spends on your site.** If your blog is a strong *referral site* to your main website, this number may be low (from a half-second to a minute or so).
- **Number of pages (posts) each visitor views.** If the page count is low, consider that some visitors may be leaving the blog to visit your company's website.
- **Referring sites.** These are the sites your blog visitors are coming from. Facebook, Twitter, and other websites where you promote your blog should be sending you visitors.
- **Keyword searches.** You can count the number of times keywords in your blog actually were typed into search engines and which keywords in your posts were most popular.

- **Most popular content.** You can gauge readers' interests by the pages they land on, where they spend most of their time, and the pages from which they exit your blog.
- **Visitors.** Use the map overlay feature to display the geographic region your traffic is coming from. For example, http://www. AtlantaRealEstateForum.com had traffic from all 50 states in a 30-day period.

Your main website's analytics also reveal how well your blog performs. An effective blog will emerge as a top referral source to the company's main website and will send quality referral traffic to the website. If your blog is separate from your website, here's what you want to look for:

- **Increased traffic.** Typically, companies will get a 20% boost in traffic or more after launching a blog and optimizing their websites, but some mRELEVANCE clients have seen growth of 200% to 600%.
- **Increase in referring sites.** Because of syndication and cross-promotion of your web presence, your blog should be among the top 5 referral sources to your main website.
- **Keywords.** The list of keywords will expand if you are blogging with keywords as anchor text.

If your blog and website arc built on the same platform you will need to gauge the ROI a bit differently. At a minimum, note keywords, time on site, and referring sites. Each of these metrics should show year-over-year increases.

You should gain at least three other measurable ROIs from your online efforts:

1. **SERP.** When you Google your name or other keyword phrases, you should start to see more of your results on page one.
2. **Enhanced brand.** Your company will be recognized as readily online as in print.
3. **Increased efficiency.** Your blog will reduce the amount of time needed to create content for your social media program by integrating your blog with your website and social media activities. Instead of posting the same material three or four times on different sites, you can write one blog post, check off the other sites where you want the material to appear, and post brief comments on social media sites between your blog posts.

With Google's release of Penguin, which is designed to penalize sites that spam the search engine to achieve higher rankings, we have been getting a lot of questions about whether the blog and website should be separate or whether the blog should be part of the website. The advantage of the latter approach is that it will continuously provide fresh content to the website. The website will be frequently indexed by the search engines, boosting SEO. The advantage of a separate blog is that as a different site it will optimize your main website through third-party SEO and *link juice*. Link juice refers to relevance or the authority that is passed to your website or blog by links (typically referred to as back links) to your site. It will also add a SERP listing that will help your reputation management campaign.

Troubleshooting

If your blog isn't a top referral source for your main website within 30–60 days of launch, one of four problems may be to blame:

1. **Infrequent posting.** When was the last time you posted? If it was 60 days ago or even three weeks ago you aren't giving your readers or the search engines a reason to come back.
2. **Dull content.** Make sure your content is compelling to your readers. Is it fun and informative? If it isn't, then spice it up!
3. **Lack of promotion.** Does your blog have an RSS feed? Did you connect it to Facebook and Twitter? Have you let your customers know where to find

it? Did you register it on blog directories? Have you sent an *e-blast* to your customers to invite them to the site?

4. **Poor construction.** Does the blog contain *hard coding* that breaks the theme? WordPress themes are a combination of files that work together to create a blog's design and functionality. Themes can be configured many ways to allow for unique design. However, if a web developer or someone else adds *HTML* code in the wrong place, your theme will not work as intended.

5. **Wrong or no SEO tools.** Make sure you have installed an SEO plug-in, like the All in One SEO plug-in. Check to see if you are using an XML sitemap plug-in as well.

Own Your Reputation

The blog is the one item in your social media toolbox that you own. Social networks will come and go. The content you post on them isn't cataloged or sortable, and, in most cases, Google doesn't index it. Most important, the content you post on social networks really isn't yours. The social media sites can (and will) change their policies and take profiles and accounts down at any time and for any reason. Even free online blog accounts are vulnerable to disappearing. Ensuring your company has a reasonable amount of control over its image and reputation becomes more and more challenging as online social media channels expand their reach.

Social Networking

ocial networking engages others in online conversation. You need the right friends, fans, and followers to network with just as you network face-to-face. Although social networking is fun, don't lose sight of your program's foundation—your blog—in the excitement of the social networking party.

Social Networking Sites

ActiveRain
Facebook
Flickr
Foursquare
Google+
Houzz
Instagram
Linkedin
Pinterest
Trulia
Tumblr
Twitter
YouTube

Facebook

Facebook is a 24/7 cocktail party with 130 (for the average Facebook user) of your closest friends. Half of Facebook users log onto the site daily. The average Facebook user is connected to 80 community pages, groups, and events. They are willing to Like your corporate fan page if you provide them with information that interests them.

Facebook is a tool for building a personal brand—or destroying your reputation. Using your personal profile, you can reconnect with old friends and make new ones. As your friends change their "status," you receive updates on your wall. Facebook users can add photos, video, and other content to their personal pages; choose their desired level of security; and build a network of connections. Before you can launch a business fan page or a group, you must first have a personal profile. Facebook is built on the premise that you are a person first and then as a person you can have a corporate page. Remember your corporation is not a person. Therefore, do not launch your corporate page as a person. Not only is this against Facebook policy, it also limits the applications you can use to interact with various audiences.

Facebook Statistics

- More than a billion monthly active users as of December 2012
- Approximately 82% of monthly active users outside the U.S. and Canada
- 618 million daily active users on average in December 2012
- 680 million monthly active users who used Facebook mobile products as of December 31, 2012[18]

Creating Your Personal Profile

Complete your profile.

- Contact information
    - Name (consider incorporating your maiden name)
    - Photo (a casual but appropriate photo is best for your profile photo)
    - Cover photo (should measure 851 pixels wide by 315 pixels tall)
    - URLs for your website, blog, Linkedin, etc.
    - Phone numbers
    - Email addresses (note: Facebook will default to your Facebook email address, unless you specify another one in your account settings)

- Current and former companies
- Education

Get your Facebook URL http://www.Facebook. com/user name (after you have 25 friends visit this page to secure the URL for your name). This is the equivalent of getting a vanity license plate. It allows you to give your custom Facebook address to your friends and business connections easily.

Customize your privacy settings. There are many levels of privacy. You can keep your profile hidden, available only to friends, or open it up to the world. Most Facebook users choose a privacy level somewhere in the middle.

Posting to Your Personal Page

After building your personal page, decide how often to post and what to post.

- Will your page be designed for friends and family?
- What content do you want to share?
- Will you post photos?

If you choose to keep your page personal, remember to share business news occasionally with your Facebook friends. You don't want to miss a great referral because one of your friends isn't thinking about what you do for a living! Whether you choose to friend personal, professional, or a combination of contacts, think carefully about what you are posting. Would you say it to your grandmother? If not, save it for a private conversation. Although you may be using Facebook's privacy settings and *direct messaging* vigorously, you are still on a public site. Always consider carefully what you intend to post online before you add content.

Encourage interaction among Facebook friends by tagging (or identifying) people in posts and in photos. To tag your post, type the @ symbol followed by a Facebook friend's name (without a space between them). For example, type @JohnDoe. Tagging causes your post to show up in the friend's feed and encourages conversations and interactions. You can also tag pages this same way. When you engage others, your information will appear more often in their feeds. If you are posting for business purposes, you want to appear in your friends' "Top News" to increase your visibility. Another way to get more interaction is to use the button in the bottom left of the "update status" box that looks like a person with a plus symbol. This allows you to post a status update or a comment and list who is with you. You can share content and spark interaction on Facebook in other ways too: add video, incorporate your blog, play a game, create an event, join causes. As you share content, you have the option of sharing it with the lists you have created. You can share some content with just friends, while other content is shared with the public.

Facebook Do's

- Use your real name and photo.
- Choose your profile photo wisely (keep it professional or neutral).
- Complete your biography thoughtfully. When you list your birthday, block the year for security reasons.
- Review your privacy settings.
- Join groups.
- Create lists.
- Consider your tone.
- Interact, comment, converse.

Facebook Don'ts

- Share personal information publicly.
- Hit "reply all" in group emails.
- Feel like you have to friend everyone, join every group, or respond to every invitation to join a page.

- Announce where you are going—*cyberstalkers* may be watching to see when you are out of town.
- Set up your business as a person.

The Fan Page

Creating a Facebook fan page gives your company the opportunity to build a fan base of people who Like your business. Once you have fans, you'll want to communicate with them regularly and find ways to engage them in conversations. Determine your audience and what to talk about. You will want to provide updates about your company, offer specials and incentives, and provide news on your latest sale. Make sure to ask for customer testimonials and consider using promotional posts or advertising on the site to increase interaction with your current fans and attract new ones.

Timeline and Photos

Facebook's timeline for pages is very similar to Timeline for user profiles with the layout including a cover photo at the top and a timeline of your page's history since its creation. Take full advantage of the timeline layout as part of your company's social media strategy. One way to do this is to add dates of important events within your company to the timeline, following these guidelines:[19]

- Size cover photos 851 pixels wide by 315 pixels tall.
- Do not include price or purchase information.
- Do not reference interface elements such as Like or Share, or any other Facebook features.
- Omit calls to action.
- Leave out contact information including email addresses, mailing addresses, and website URLs.

  Here's what you can do:

- Post a photo or collage of photos of your most popular products.
- Show a photo of people using/interacting with your product.
- Highlight unique features or positive statistics about your company.
- Include your *tagline*.

Maintaining the Page

Page administrators have more control over pages than ever. They can highlight, hide, or delete stories from timelines. The Admin panel shows the latest notifications, newest page likes, and the insights graph. It also includes a Manage section where an administrator can edit the page, use the activity log, or see banned users; a Build Audience section where administrators can invite email contacts or friends and share the page with others; and a Help section. You can also use the Facebook Page App. It allows you to manage your branded Facebook page from your smartphone. You can post, comment, and respond easily from your phone, so you can manage your page on-the-go.

Communicating and Getting Fans

Having the right fans is critical to success with Facebook. Think about the target audience(s) with whom you can successfully interact on Facebook, seek them out, and start conversations with them. Make sure to include existing customers, who will comprise much of your Facebook audience. Since your customers will be your best brand advocates, give them reasons to stay and interact.

There *is* such a thing as a free lunch, or there should be if you are a restaurant owner seeking fans and new customers on Facebook. Slope's BBQ of Cartersville, Georgia (http://www.facebook.com/SlopesBBQof Cartersville), posts specials, offers, and weekly contests on its page, including a free lunch for a "fan of the week." This helps the restaurant engage potential customers and interact with existing customers to get repeat business. Simply having a profile on Facebook and pushing your messages out isn't enough to build your brand, though. You need a team member who fully embraces the medium. He or she could be the president of the company, *online sales counselor,* receptionist, marketing director, salesperson, or a family member. As you build your Facebook presence, the leader of your effort should strive to find three to five new fans daily and interact with them. As your presence solidifies, find creative ways to engage the fans that Like you in conversation on your Facebook wall. Slope's BBQ uses promoted posts and Facebook advertising to make sure its fans see content. The owner, Mark, posts to the page daily and interacts with fans (fig. 4.1).

Creating Your Fan Page

Choose your category carefully because it will determine what options are available on your About page. Your choice may be different from other similar businesses. Some options are

- local business or place;
- company, organization, or institution;
- brand or product;
- artist, band, or public figure;
- entertainment; or
- cause or community.

Figure 4.1 **Slopes BBQ**

Slope's restaurant rewards a "fan of the week" with a free lunch. (Source: Reprinted with permission from Slopes BBQ, Cartersville, Georgia)

Also choose your name thoughtfully. Facebook suggests choosing a name as close as possible to your business name. Your Facebook page will typically appear in Google search results for your name, so it can improve your page one search results.

Building Out the Fan Page

Include your logo as your profile photo and a photo for your timeline cover, and complete the About section with your website URL, phone numbers, business hours, and links to your other social media sites.

Then thoroughly build out your page with the following:

- **A blog.** Use Networked Blogs, RSS Graffiti, or notes to connect your blog so your blog posts appear on your Facebook wall.
- **Video.** Upload video directly to your site or add it via YouTube or another video application. Visitors like visuals. Short videos are the perfect way to demonstrate your products and services. Consider adding customer testimonials too.
- **Photos.** Add photos directly to your page or to albums organized by topic (people love viewing pictures of products, events, and other buyers).
- **Tabs.** Add tabs to your Facebook page to greatly expand your ability to interact with fans who Like your page. You can build tabs using HTML, *JavaScript*, or *CSS*. For those with less technical know-how, Facebook has built-in applications (some free and some fee based) to help you create a tab. Facebook has changed how it will handle these pages. Stay up to date on new requirements by reading blogs, such as http://www.Mashable.com, that follow and blog about Facebook changes.

Finding Fans

After you build your page, add content, and write status updates, you must find fans. Most Facebook users will visit your page to review it for relevant content before they decide whether or not to Like it. You may want to provide an incentive for them to Like your page. From a $10 coupon to a percentage discount on their next purchase, companies are finding fun ways to reward and encourage fans to Like them on Facebook. According to *Advertising Age*, Facebook has become the "loyalty card of the Internet."[20] Give your buyers ways to embrace you. From the "Build Audience" tab you can promote your Facebook fan page to friends and prospective clients in four primary ways:

1. **Invite email contacts.** Choose which email service you want to use to invite your contacts, or upload an existing list to Facebook.
2. **Invite friends.** As a page administrator, you can invite any of your personal friends to Like the page. Once they Like your Fan page you will not be able to click them; this prevents you from asking them more than once.
3. **Share page.** Write a comment, such as "Please Like my page for great incentives." Choose who you want to share with from the drop-down arrow to the right of "on your own timeline" (options are: on

your own timeline, on a friend's timeline, in a group, on your page, in a private message). Click **share page.**

4. **Create an Ad.** You can promote your page, an event, an application, a domain, or a specific post on your page. You can even promote who likes your page to their friends! After you choose what to promote, you can also choose your audience. Available options include location, age, gender, interests, categories, and connections. You will need to determine your advertising objective and set a budget.

You can promote your Facebook page with coupons and contests. Companies have created clever campaigns to get various audiences to Like their pages to download a coupon or win a gift card. This strategy, combined with e-blasts and blog promotions, can quickly build a fan base. Always comply with Facebook policies[21] and your state's sweepstakes laws if you run contests and campaigns. Also, promotions must be administered within apps on Facebook.com. This can be a Canvas page or a Page app. Promotions must completely release Facebook from liability and state that Facebook does not sponsor the promotion. In addition, you cannot use Facebook features or functionality as a promotions registration mechanism. In other words, you cannot use the act of liking a page to register a person for a contest. Also, you cannot notify winners through Facebook.

Mention your page on the pages of related groups or on other corporate pages. When you join a group or Like a corporate page, you can usually post to its wall. This is a great way to cross-promote upcoming events, but know the group's policies before posting. Group moderators may consider your post spam and delete it, or they may report you to Facebook.

After your page has 25 fans, you can get your fan page URL. Go to http://www.Facebook.com/user name to secure a unique name. This is important for two reasons: (1) the search engines index page URLs—you want yours to appear when prospective buyers search for your name, and (2) you can add the URL to your printed collateral.

You also may want to explore Facebook groups. If you host many events, a group page may serve you better than a fan page. However, most companies find that a fan page offers the best options to achieve their broad social media marketing goals. The two types of Facebook pages offer slightly different functionality.

American Standard (the plumbing products manufacturer) worked with its public relations agency, O'Reilly-DePalmato to increase the former company's number of Facebook followers through contests and sweepstakes. The strategy worked; a bathroom make-over contest tripled its Facebook fan base.

The brand had already built awareness around an annual contest aimed at consumers: the American Standard Ugliest Bathroom Contest. Previous promotions had been costly, using custom-built web pages but offered no opportunity for American Standard to interact with contestants vying for a beautiful new American Standard bathroom worth $20,000.

Facebook was a budget-friendly solution for contest entrants to upload images and text, because O'Reilly-DePalma used Wildfire, a third-party app, as the contest platform, in compliance with Facebook's rules. The agency provided art direction for the graphics execution, selecting compelling "before" pictures from previous contest winners to encourage submissions. Other promotion was through social media. No paid advertising was used. The results were impressive!

- Facebook fans increased threefold. The company retained these fans even after the contest closed.
- The company's e-newsletter added 400 subscribers.
- Of the entries received in the top round, four finalists selected by American Standard executives got more than 2,700 people engaged with the

contest and the brand in their quest to earn the most votes to win the beautiful new bathroom.

- Final before-and-after stories, photos, and videos were covered in a feature story on a magazine's website.

For the next phase of growth, American Standard tried a Facebook-based sweepstakes. Sweepstakes are different from contests, in that sweepstakes are chance-based (like a lottery ticket) and contests involve a level of judging. For the sweepstakes, the company promoted the contest with $600 in Facebook advertising and the brand marketing team posted the opportunity in digital communities that track sweepstakes and giveaways.

The sweepstakes generated more than 5,500 entries, with impressive results: Facebook Likes increased fivefold in three weeks, and were retained after the sweepstakes ended.

Social media skeptics might be asking how these activities and others like them translate to sales and profits. But that's like trying to tie sales to a single advertisement or story placement through public relations, which is normally not possible. However, these activities attracted consumers to the American Standard circle of influence, where they were exposed to the brand's products and key messages, increasing the chances that when it came time to make a bathroom purchase, the American Standard brand was positioned favorably among consumers' choices.

Facebook Events

Creating events on Facebook is fun and easy. From the Events tab on your fan page, click **create event.** Include details such as contact information for visitors who have questions, whether there is a fee to participate in the event, and whether it requires an RSVP (and how to respond if payment is required). You can choose to show the guest list on the event page or keep it private. You also can choose to allow guests to post to the event wall, or only permit administrators to.

Promoting Your Facebook Page

After you have a Facebook page, tell people about it by listing your Facebook page on your website, blog, email signature, Linkedin page, and in other communications. You can use the Facebook icon or include a text link to the page. Other ways to promote your Facebook page are by writing about it on your blog, discussing it in your email newsletter, and adding it to your advertising.

Getting Fans

Buyers Like you on Facebook because they want something. You will keep them as fans if you continue to provide reasons to Like you. You could announce your events and sales on Facebook first, or provide fans with a coupon or special incentive such as a discount off their first purchase, or a buy one get one free, or even something they can share with a friend. Lakeland, Florida-based Highland Homes created a Facebook coupon that encouraged visitors to Like its page (fig. 4.2). The coupon offered a 10% to 20% discount on options from the company's Personal Selection Studio, depending on when buyers purchased their new homes. Twelve coupons were redeemed.

S&A Homes launched a similar promotion in August 2010. Home shoppers could Like the S&A Homes page on Facebook and download a coupon for $1,500 toward the purchase of options. The coupon and the Facebook page launched at approximately the same time to create a buzz. Six buyers downloaded and redeemed the coupons.

In addition, some S&A Homes buyers have liked the builder's page after signing a contract. This is a good way to encourage referrals through social media.

When S&A Homes launched its Facebook page (fig. 4.3), the company strategically targeted real estate

Figure 4.2 Highland Homes Facebook page

Highland Homes posts and interacts daily with prospects and agents on its Facebook page. (Source: Reprinted with permission from Highland Homes, Lakeland, Florida)

agents to Like the page—and more than 100 did so within weeks. Again, the company offered an incentive—a $10 Sheetz gas card. To participate, agents simply had to Like the page and write on its wall. The campaign promoted S&A's blog, email messages (fig. 4.4), and of course, its Facebook page.

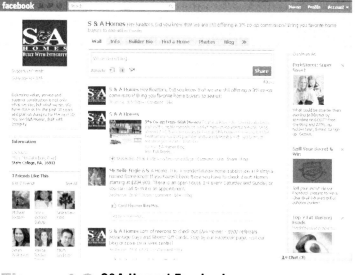

Figure 4.3 S&A Homes' Facebook page

S&A Homes promotes its incentives and specials on its Facebook page. (Source: Reprinted with permission from S&A Homes, State College, Pennsylvania)

Comments posted on the wall included "Great quality and great people!" and "Sold 2 S&A Homes . . . easy to work with and both clients were very pleased." Wall posters even complimented specific employees for customer service.

S&A HOMES E-INCENTIVE FOR REALTORS!

S&A Homes hopes to put some "**drive**" back into the economy and a few lucky Realtors will be able to put some gas in their tanks. Our new E-Incentive offers the first 200 Realtors who "like" our S&A Homes corporate Facebook page a **$10 Sheetz gift card**.

E-Incentive Directions:
Realtors, if you want to receive a $10 Sheetz gift card, here are the steps:

1. Log into your Facebook account
2. "Like" the S&A Homes' corporate page @ www.facebook.com/sahomes
3. Post one thing you love about S&A Homes.

After you have signed up and posted a message, a representative will contact you directly to mail your gift card.

www.facebook.com/sahomes

www.sahomesblog.com

Figure 4.4 **Sheetz email incentive**

The Sheetz $10 gift card incentive encouraged Realtors to Like the S&A Homes Facebook page and write on its wall (Source: Reprinted with permission from S&A Homes, State College, Pennsylvania)

Twitter

Twitter is a *microblog* that allows users to, in essence, send text messages or instant messages (IMs) to the world. Twitter users send and receive tweets (messages) of no more than 140 characters. Your followers can log onto http://www.Twitter.com to see your *timeline* of tweets. People will decide whether they want to follow you based on your profile and the content of your tweets. If all of your tweets are push marketing—your events, your product, your stuff—readers will quickly lose interest. Consider your frustration with email spam like "Be number one on Google," "Join my multilevel marketing program," "Buy this great drug without a prescription from Canada." Folks are bombarded with these same messages on Twitter, so don't add to the spam by constantly pushing your products and services.

You may want to set up multiple accounts on Twitter. Many businesses have a company account managed by multiple people, and separate accounts for individual team members, including one for the president, CEO, or other public figure that represents the company. Carefully consider the best way to create these accounts before building them. Each company has a unique marketing culture. If you create a corporate account, you should include the Twitter bio of anyone tweeting for the company. Go to https://twitter.com/DeltaAssist, http://Twitter.com/GerstadBuilders, or https://twitter.com/comcast for three approaches for showing who is tweeting for your company.

About Twitter

- More than 500 million registered users as of 2012
- Generates more than 340 million tweets daily
- Handles more than 1.6 billion search queries per day
- One of the 10 most visited websites on the Internet[22]

Creating a Twitter Account

To create a Twitter account, go to https://twitter.com/ and enter your name (or company name), email address, and desired user name. Choose a name that will help users locate your company. Twitter allows 15 characters for your name. If you are Michael Robin, choose your name rather than a generic alternative like MR846, for example, so people can find you. For your business, I recommend using your company name. Your name and your user name can be identical. The username will appear in your Twitter URL. For example, if you want to find me, my url is https://twitter.com/AtlantaPR.

After you create your account, the Twitter Teacher will help you set up features. The first step is to build your timeline. This is where you will be able to view the tweets of all the Twitter users you follow. The Teacher suggests following five people. (You can follow my accounts: @AtlantaPR, @mRELEVANCE, and @AtlantaREForum.) After you follow the first five, the teacher suggests you find five others. It will also suggest searching your email contacts for others to follow. You should upload an image of yourself (a photo or your company logo)—rather than an avatar, your child, your dog, or the default Twitter egg—and a bio (either personal or company). Your bio should be fun. People are much more likely to follow interesting people and companies than just another "me too." Don't forget to include your location (city and state) and website URL. After completing these steps you can start tweeting and building an audience of followers. People will choose to follow you and your company based on your profile and your tweets. They may not think you are a real person if your profile is incomplete or if you have never tweeted.

Twitter Terminology

Direct messages. You can easily send a personal message to one of your followers or another Twitter user, similar to sending an email message:

1. **Select** your "me" page from the top navigation bar. Click the direct message icon under your Twitter banner image (it looks like an envelope). From this window you can reply to a direct message or start a new message. To start a new message, begin typing the recipient's Twitter handle. A drop-down list opens. Select the name of the user you want to message. Type your message in the conversation box.

2. You can also send a direct message from your home page on Twitter. Type a capital D followed by a space in front of a user's Twitter handle in the "compose a new Tweet" conversation box, and then add your message.

You can also use a Twitter app to perform the Direct Message function seamlessly. My favorite is Tweet Deck, which is owned by Twitter. It allows you to load multiple Twitter accounts into one Tweet Deck so you can see mentions, followers, direct messages, lists, and more on one screen.

Hashtag. The pound sign (#); provides a method to categorize tweets, search for specific subjects, and track trends. You can search Twitter without using the hashtag, but many people still use it to organize content, especially for conferences and conventions. For example, the International Builders' Show hashtag is #IBSVegas. When you perform a search for the hashtag you find everyone attending the conference and tweeting about the show. It is a great way to meet people and find others with similar interests.

Retweet (RT). Sending a tweet from another user; similar to forwarding an email message.

Modified Tweet (MT). Shortening a tweet to save space while trying to preserve its meaning.

Partial Retweet (PRT). Similar to a modified tweet, a partial retweet indicates something was left out to save space so the person retweeting can add their spin to it.

User name. The name, or Twitter handle, under which an individual's or company's tweets will appear, such as @AtlantaPR. The corresponding Twitter URL is http://Twitter.com/AtlantaPR.

Tweeting With Personality

You have only 140 characters to make your point. For maximum impact, keep your tweets conversational, retweetable, and fun. What you say doesn't have to be personal, but it should have personality. Reserve about 30 characters of your tweet so readers who Like it can easily comment on and retweet it. This means that you really only have about 110 characters per tweet. You can

- tweet about your business;
- provide tips (seasonal home care, best remodeling projects, landscaping ideas);
- share news (tax credits, mortgage rates, incentives);
- retweet other content; and
- ask questions and engage in conversations.

Of course, if you are tweeting from Tweet Deck (or other Twitter apps), you can tweet longer updates by using Deck.ly, or other similar tweet shorteners. However, most people expect short messages on Twitter, so don't overuse long updates.

Add your location, a photo, or video. Reference an article. Vary your message. Make sure that you are having conversations on Twitter and not just promoting your products and services.

No more than 25% of your tweets should be about yourself or your company. Aim for a ratio of 1:4 of tweets about yourself or your company to other tweets. Include URLs, photos, videos, and links to your website or blog.

You should shorten long URLs to save space when tweeting. Many Twitter applications (such as Tweet Deck and Hoot Suite) already do this, but if you are tweeting directly on Twitter, you can use http://www.TinyURL.com or www.Bitly.com to shorten URLs.

Following are some Tweets from home builders I follow. They demonstrate a mix of promotion and engagement.

@BooneHomes

Want to save 38.1% on your energy bill? Our Richmond new homes with Energy Star features can help http://bit.ly/gXeEGM

@BooneHomes

Sweet!! Spring is almost here! Time to paint that used home . . . unless you live in a Boone Homes No maintenance community.

@LancasterHomes

RT @aftanfisher: This is my house!! Thanks @Lancasterhomes http://yfrog.com/hs5ltypj

@abqbuilder

If home is where the heart is, why would you want to go with the cheapest bidder?

@LennarAtlanta

We just hit more than 9,000 upload views on our YouTube channel. Want to help us reach 10,000? http://bit.ly/9FHqjo

@LennarAtlanta

Confirmed @Reformationbrew will be providing some of their new product for tasting at #OTPtweetup be among the 1st! http://bit.ly/g8bkaI

Following People

If you're already on Twitter, are you following customers who will buy from you? Or are you only following others in the industry? Even worse, do you automatically follow everyone who follows you? If so, most of your "followers" are probably *bots* (robots that automate Internet tasks) or spammers. You must follow the right people on Twitter.

The right people are influencers who interact with you to widen your influence, and consumers who either will buy from you or who will influence others to buy from you. How do you find the right people? Sometimes finding one person and reviewing his or her list of followers will help you to find 10 more followers (birds of a feather flock together). Home builders will probably want to follow real estate agents and remodelers may want to start by following their best referral sources. Local businesses will want to follow consumers in their localized area. Develop the strategy you think will work best for your company and then review its effectiveness after 30, 60, and 90 days.

Searching for Followers

Review the followers of your influencers. These may be real estate agents, vendors, or just friends. Observe who your target market is following, including competitors.

- Use the People Search function on Twitter. (You must know exactly who you are looking for.)
- Search for profile types using the advanced search on Twitter.
- Search Twellow (http://www.twellow.com) for related profiles.
- Use Tweepz (http://www.tweepz.com) to find matching profiles.

Participating in online events that use hashtags will also increase your followers. For example, I sometimes participate in #blogchat and #Linkedinchat. Twitter chats provide an opportunity to meet new people with similar interests from around the country, and share expertise.

Once you have followers you'll want to build *lists*.[23] If you are following 500 or 1,000 people it can be hard to keep up with all the tweets you want to read because the Twitter *stream* moves so rapidly. Lists help you isolate specific groups so you can see more of what you want to read. Remember that lists only allow you to read tweets. You cannot send tweets to a list en masse. You can include users you are not following (as long as they have not blocked you) in your lists to keep up with their tweets, which is a stealthy way to monitor your competitors. For example, you can build lists for a local area, your sales force, suppliers, and competitors. This allows you to sort tweets. Consider locking your lists if you don't want to share that great group of city-specific real estate agents you've spent time building.

Customize Your Twitter Background

Twitter is a branding opportunity, as well as a communications vehicle, for your company. Even if you choose a basic background, use your corporate colors. You can get the *hexadecimal code* for the colors from your website designer so you can match them precisely. If you want to extend branding on Twitter, hire a graphic artist to create a custom background for your page.

Twitter now offers a header image similar to Facebook's timeline image. This means that you have the ability to brand your background, header image, and avatar on your Twitter page. Use these specifications:

- **Header image**—Original image size 1,252 × 626 pixels (maximum file size 5MB). Twitter does not specify a minimum size, but anything smaller than 640 pixels wide may not display well.

- **Avatar**—128 × 128 square (scales to 48 × 48 in the stream of tweets). Use your logo or portrait photo.
- **Background**—To reach most users, use images of 66 × 194 pixels for the left side of your Twitter profile background. Twitter content has a fixed width of 865 pixels, which leaves the remainder for backgrounds. When designing your new Twitter background, consider placing important information about your company, such as your website URL and phone number, on the left side of your template so people who visit your page can easily contact you by phone or find your website. You can also include branding and a call to action in your header image. When designing this image feel free to announce your latest sale, use your tag line, promote your URL, and sell your product or service. You could even include an arrow pointing to your phone number with text that says, "Click Here!"

Twitter Do's

- Choose a name that makes sense.
- Complete your entire profile.
- Follow people whom you want to follow you.

- Retweet others' interesting tweets.
- Ask questions and engage in conversation.
- Start slowly by following a number of accounts and spend time just reading and listening.
- Twitter is a tool for immediate conversation, not what happened 12 hours ago. Respond to "@" replies and direct messages as you receive them.
- Build lists of followers to allow you to break through the clutter and focus on specific groups.
- Tweet regularly.

Twitter Don'ts

- Read every message that your followers post; you will never catch up.
- Use Twitter for blatant self promotion. Instead, share useful information, build a relationship, converse.
- Forget that when you write something online, it lasts forever. If you wouldn't say it in real life, don't tweet it.
- Tweet about mundane events (we don't care what you ate for breakfast).
- Lash out if you are attacked by a follower. Instead think about the appropriate response and when you do respond, be transparent and honest.

- Engage *trolls*. Trolls post off-topic messages that are usually hurtful, controversial, or inflammatory on Twitter, Facebook, blogs, or other social sites.

Twitter Applications

Applications help you manage multiple accounts from one location. They have built-in URL shortening, allow users to create groups of followers, sort through numerous tweets quickly, and see all columns, including lists, on one screen.

Twitter apps for smartphones allow you to tweet on-the-go. Even if you don't yet have a smartphone, you can still text tweets from a cell phone. Integrating Twitter into your daily routine makes it less an interruption and more a habit you are likely to maintain. I may check tweets on my iPhone while cleaning stalls in my barn or on the way to dinner (with someone else driving of course!).

For PC or Mac, try TweetDeck, HootSuite, Seesmic, or SocialOomph. For smartphones, try HootSuite, TwitterBerry, Tweetie, or TweetDeck. I like the main Twitter application for iPhone and iPad. It is a clean interface that works well.

Twitter Searches

Monitor Twitter conversations. You need to know what others are saying about you and your brand. Here are some quick and easy ways to do this:

- Search any company name or phrase to find out what's currently on Twitter by using http://search.Twitter.com.
- From your Twitter home page, check to see who is mentioning you: click **@Connect** in the top navigation. You have the options of looking at Interactions or Mentions. Interactions show everyone who has recently followed you, as well as the conversations you've had with others. Just click on "view conversation" to see an entire transcript of a recent conversation. Mentions include the list of everyone who has tweeted and mentioned your Twitter handle. Monitor these tweets carefully because they may contain questions about your business.
- Create automated searches using your Twitter app (like TweetDeck). At a minimum, create these for your company's name and your name.
- Use Google Alerts (http://www.google.com/alerts), a free service, to set up alerts for your name, your company, and even your competitors.

Promote your Twitter Account

Promote your Twitter account as you do your Facebook page. List your Twitter account on your website, blog, email signature, Facebook page, and other communications using the Twitter icon or a link in your text. To maximize the effectiveness of Twitter, invest time to find followers, post content, and engage in conversation.

YouTube

YouTube is a video-sharing network with user profiles and channels. Consumers can view your products and services. You can show an active portrayal of what your company does or educate consumers with a how-to video. One of my friends learned how to knit by watching YouTube videos.

You can make the videos private so only select users can view them, or you can make them publicly available. Storing videos for all of your websites on YouTube helps prevent clogging up your server and hogging bandwidth. Load videos on YouTube and link to them from your blog, website, Facebook page, Twitter account, and other locations. Search engines love video, so an account on YouTube will boost your SEO and ranking in the SERPs.

YouTube Statistics

- More than 800 million unique users visit YouTube each month.
- More than 4 billion hours of video are watched each month on YouTube.
- 72 hours of video are uploaded to YouTube every minute.
- 70% of YouTube traffic comes from outside the US.
- YouTube is localized in 53 countries and across 61 languages.
- In 2011, YouTube had more than 1 trillion views or around 140 views for every person on Earth[24].

Setting Up the Account

Go to http://www.youtube.com and click **Sign In** at the top right corner of the home page. The next screen will give you the option to sign in or to create a new account. To create a new account, enter a Google user name, password, and your name, birthdate, gender, mobile phone number, and an email address. To finalize the registration process you will need to enter the *CAPTCHA* text to prove you are not a robot, and confirm your location and agree to Google Terms of Service and Privacy Policy.

On the next screen, you can create your Google Profile, which will also create your Google+ account (discussed in more detail later in this chapter). Or you can skip this step and create a YouTube profile instead.

Complete the entire profile, including a description and your website URL. Your user name will be part of your YouTube URL. For example, the user name "JohnDoe" would result in a profile URL of http://www.youtube.com/user/johndoe. If you need technical help, visit http://www.Google.com/support/youtube/.

Customize your channel:

- Enter a channel title. You can insert spaces between words.
- Add channel tags. Include your company name and other keywords.
- Add themes and colors. Choose from the standard options or use the advanced options to fully customize your channel.

Choose what to display, from comments to friends to recent activity in the modules. This is what others will see when they visit your channel.

Start Uploading

Now you can upload videos! Title each one with a *keyword-optimized title,* choose a thumbnail, and add a description and tags (YouTube's term for keywords) to help search engines find the video. In addition to posting videos, you can subscribe to other YouTube user profiles, join groups, and create lists of favorite videos. This will help increase your company's visibility on YouTube. When consumers visit other profiles and see your icon, they are likely to click through to see your videos and may subscribe to your content.

Enhance Your Video

Under the edit section of a video, you can do more than just add information and settings. You can add enhancements, audio, annotations, and captions.

- Enhancements allow you to add filters to your video, automatically correct lighting and stability, and edit the video in other ways.
- Audio enables editors to include audio tracks within their video.
- Annotation offers a way to overlay text and links on your video. The annotations section gives you the option of adding speech bubbles, notes, titles, spotlights, labels, and links to certain other pages

including another video, playlist, channel, sub-scription page, or fund-raising project.
* Captions provide a way to add more explanation to your video to help viewers follow along.

YouTube Tips

Observe how other companies use YouTube. Viewers will share funny, entertaining, or informative videos with others.

* Keep videos short—90 seconds to 2 minutes.
* Use a digital camcorder or your smartphone to capture videos. (You don't necessarily need a professional to shoot video, although you may want to hire one for specific projects.)
* Post virtual tours of your products and services.
* Post quick tours privately for remote clients.
* Enlist customers to shoot testimonial videos for you.

Helping Customers Visualize

Central Florida home builder Highland Homes began shooting videos of homes three years ago to increase customer satisfaction. The company builds over a wide geographic region and wanted its customers to be able to see finished homes from plans regardless of whether they were under construction in a particular local area.

To help customers visualize the completed homes, a motivated agent recorded video tours of finished homes from each floor plan.

The videos made the sales presentation go much more smoothly because customers could view a high-definition video of a floor plan on the spot. It eliminated the need to give prospects a $25 gas card incentive to drive to models in remote locations.

Kathie McDaniel, MIRM, MCSP, a real estate broker and vice president of sales and marketing for Highland Homes, says the company uses a professional videographer to record examples of all of its floor plans, as the homes are built, to add to the builder's library (fig. 4.5). The company also has added videos of its Personal Selection Studio to YouTube. Buyers who view the clips prior to making selections are more prepared to choose home options and they request fewer change orders than those who haven't viewed these videos, she says.

As online video viewing continues to boom, the Equifax® Finance Blog (blog.equifax.com) is staying competitive and looking for better ways to get its name and message to consumers using video marketing.

The site offers a wealth of money management resources with frequent posts, tips, and discussions on how to make your money go further. To engage readers, take advantage of the power of online videos, and boost the site's search engine ranking and number of users,

Figure 4.5 **Highland Homes YouTube channel**

Highland Homes created a library of videos that allows people to take virtual home tours and select options. (Source: Reprinted with permission from Highland Homes, Lakeland, Florida)

the Equifax Finance Blog launched the Equifax Family Money Matters Video contest for its followers. The contest helped increase site traffic, improve page rank, and make one of its lucky followers $1,000 richer.

The contest asked site visitors to create, submit, and share with Equifax readers a YouTube video about strategies they use to save money. Video contests are especially effective marketing projects because they are personal. Each submission becomes part of your marketing collateral as contestants share their videos among family, friends, and others in their network to garner enough votes to win your contest.

For the Equifax Family Money Matters Video contest, winners were selected by popular vote from blog readers (one vote per person per day over a two-week period). The top five finalists received a free one-year subscription to Equifax's newest credit monitoring product, Equifax Complete™ Family Plan, and the grand prize winner received a $1,000 Discover Gift Card.

The Equifax Finance Blog promoted the contest using all of its social sites. Each video received several hundred votes, quadrupling the number of visitors to the site during the contest period. The winning and finalist videos were announced on the site to provide practical personal finance tips to blog readers.

Podcasting

Podcasting is a way to deliver digital media to users. They can subscribe to your content and download it to a computer or mobile device. You can deliver audio, video, PDF, or ePub files through podcasts. I started Atlanta Real Estate Forum Radio as a podcast in October of 2011 with Dreamland Interactive LLC and my friend and co-host Todd Schnick. The show has proven to be a great outreach tool in the Atlanta real estate market and has helped us promote our blog to new readers, as well as reach an entirely new audience of iTunes listeners.

With the explosive growth of smartphones and tablets, and the increasing focus on mobile computing and content consumption, audio and video content such as podcasts and YouTube videos are more popular than ever. They are easy to produce and just as easy for consumers to find and consume. The proliferation of social sharing, blogs, and apps makes it easier for consumers to find your show. Tagging your podcasts with the right keywords enables the search engines to find your content.

After building a subscriber base for your show, as with any new consumer, you want to get them to come back for more content. This can happen many ways, such as having them sign up for additional content like email lists, webinars, e-book downloads, videos, or other products.

How many subscribers should you aim for? That depends on your goals and your marketing plan. If you only need one buyer to make a difference, you don't need tens of thousands of listeners; you only need to target the right audience for your content. If you are trying to sell thousands of products, you need a much larger audience.

Each day brings innovations, more distribution channels, and new technologies that expand the range of possibilities for sharing audio and video content. As I type this, platforms are emerging that will be to podcasts what Netflix is to films. The possibilities are endless. Smartphones and tablets have changed the ball game. The on-demand nature of content means that people can click play to listen to your content whenever and wherever it is convenient. Apps and mobile websites that showcase audio and video content are being developed and launched each day. Listeners can select the kind of content they want to consume and have it delivered directly to them. They can receive notifications when new material has been published. Most importantly, they've given you permission to send them this new content so you have a willing and hungry audience.

"Podcasting is a great way to create content. Lots of people aren't comfortable writing but they are happy to talk," says my co-host, Todd. "You have to think about four things when launching an online show: goals, content (guest recruitment), distribution, and production."

Goals

Is your show's goal to generate good content, thereby educating your market and growing the audience for your marketing platform? Is your show about business development? Or, is your show about some combination of the two?

Don't overlook the business development aspect of your podcast. Reaching out to people for interviews is a great way to connect with people (prospects and partners) who are potentially important to your business.

Content

So what are you going to podcast about? Is the content going to educate your market? Entertain your market? Will you produce the content alone to share your knowledge? Or will you feature interviews and conversation with other market influencers?

Your podcast becomes a critical component to your content marketing program (which draws more people you can convert to buyers). Moreover, don't overlook the positive SEO value of publishing podcast and video content to the web. The search engines always like fresh content that people are linking to and sharing.

Distribution

How are you going to spread the word about your podcast? You can tap into directories such as iTunes or plug into smartphone apps like Stitcher, both with audiences in the tens of thousands that are looking for specific content to learn from, and to kill time while stuck in traffic or exercising on the treadmill. You can promote the content on your blog, social media, and through your email marketing mailing list; or incorporate all of these options.

The content generated on your show becomes great interactive information for your existing platform and becomes a beacon that will draw new consumers. People consume content in many different ways. Some like to read, some like to watch videos, and some like to listen to audio when they are on the train, in the car, or at the gym. The more helpful content you offer, the more likely you are to interest a prospect in wanting to learn more. And as they share your content, especially helpful and interactive content that is different from a typical written blog post, you become exposed to more people interested in learning what you have to say. As with other facets of business, success in podcasting requires perseverance and consistently providing good content. If you do this, your audience will grow. Posting one or two podcasts won't draw in a crowd. Success here, as with many tactical marketing options, depends on an ongoing strategy. The more content you share, the faster you will grow your audience exponentially by word of mouth. Our radio show, Atlanta Real Estate Forum Radio has grown steadily each and every month since its inception.

Production

Finally, you can record and produce your podcast very inexpensively by using free tools, apps, and open-source platforms available on the Internet. You can record your audio by using the voice recorder apps that come with most phones, or by downloading an app called SoundCloud. You can then edit your audio podcasts using GarageBand (on Apple), or with a free download called Audacity (where we edit the Atlanta Real Estate Forum Radio show). You can publish direct to iTunes (for free), or to Stitcher. Producing and publishing audio content has never been simpler or less expensive.

Moreover, offering your guests a richer radio interview experience, one that takes place in a real studio, is easy to attain as well. Most radio stations will rent studio space upon request. This will obviously be more expensive than using free Internet apps, but will provide a more memorable experience for your guests. You can hire professionals to do your post-production work such as editing and processing. Find them locally or via Internet contracting sites such as oDesk or ELance.

The end result should provide interactive content to benefit your listeners, educate your market, build trust and rapport with your audience, and build or enhance business relationships with your guests.

You don't need a communications background, journalism degree, technical savvy, or a voice like Jimmy Baron to succeed in podcasting. In fact, you just need the ability to strike up a conversation with another person.

The interest in audio content has never been higher. According to Edison Research,[25] 36 million Americans listen to podcasts each month. And the trend is growing, thanks to the smartphone, which provides easy on-demand access to the content. And as suggested by the recent Google algorithm updates, search engines like Google are emphasizing digital content such as podcasts, videos, and blogs more than ever. To be competitive in the digital age, you need to produce original content.

Google+

Google+ (http://www.plus.google.com) is a social networking site owned and operated by Google. More than 500 million users were registered for Google+ in 2012. Google+ offers users, among other features, ways to share content, explore hot topics, create events, share photos, and connect with businesses. For businesses, Google+ has become an even more essential social media tool now that it has merged Google Business pages with Google+ Local and Google Places.

Interacting

Although it's great to have a profile and add a button to your website, the purpose of any social media network is to interact. Businesses can share updates, photos, videos, links, and events with the world or with specific circles. Each item of content created on the site is displayed with a +1 button. This button allows others to, in essence, "like" your content and share it with others. Because reciprocity is key to effective social networking (and business success), businesses should use +1 to share content from others.

What Google Local Features Mean to Your Company

Even if potential customers don't know you exist, they can still find your company. Let's say you own an Italian restaurant. If a customer does a Google Local search for "Italian food" the top restaurants that provide Italian food in the area will be listed. Users can then view reviews that other Google+ users have posted as well as reviews by their friends and followers. After reading the great reviews about your business the user can instantly get directions using Google Maps. Keep in mind that all of this can be done from a user's phone, allowing you to reach out-of-town customers. Google Local has the potential to become the top business review service online. It is now easier than ever for customers to find your business online and share reviews about your company with their friends and followers. If your company never created a Google Places account you can claim your business by visiting Google Places for Business.

The social impact of Google+ is just as promising. Google Local has the potential to help your business to go viral through social media like never before. Now that Google+ users can give your business's posts a +1 and share reviews about your company, their followers can read their review, and comment on that review for all of their followers to see as well. Clicks on +1 are becoming part of Google's search algorithm, so getting more followers in your circles to click +1 on your posts pushes your website higher in search engine rankings. Google is trying to establish a connection between you, your content, and your likes online. Your Google+ profile helps the search engine deliver relevant results to you based on your behavior.

Google+ allows businesses to interact with users at the user's request, rather than littering their pages with annoying business ads like other social media platforms. Whether or not Google Local becomes popular, there is no reason not to create a Places account for your business. Why miss out on potential customers or squander Google's SEO value? Signing up for Google Places is easy and free.

Creating an Account

If you already have a Gmail address, setting up your Google+ account is easy. You can find your Google+ page on your Google toolbar or visit the URL directly. You'll be asked to build your circles with friends, family, and other people you may know or who are in your Gmail address book. Complete your personal profile as follows:

- Enter all personal information.
- Add a profile photo.
- Add a cover photo.

Creating a Business Page

After your personal profile is complete, create a page for your business by visiting http://www.plus.google.com/pages.

- Pick a category for your page. You have several choices:
  - Local Business or Place
  - Product or Brand
  - Company, Institution, or Organization
  - Arts, Entertainment, or Sports (this category includes movies, TV, music, books, sports, shows, and blogs)
  - Other (if your page doesn't fit existing categories)
- Make your page come alive. Add a cover photo, logo, and description of the page. You can preview your page and make changes as you complete it.
- If you are a local business, you'll be asked to provide your location and phone number so Google can find your company in Google Places.

- Update your profile information thoroughly and use keywords.
- After creating your page, Google offers quick tips to maximize it. You may want to click through these to learn more about how to use your Google page account, where to check and view your complete profile, and how to share information.
- Google displays a slider on your home page that allows you to choose the frequency of the posts you will see in your home stream—from nothing that anyone in your circles posts to everything posted within your circles.

Adding People to Your Circles

From your personal Google+ page you can follow other brands, businesses, and your customers. To follow customers from your page, they will first have to add your page to a circle. Likewise, you can search for business pages to add to your circles. Default circles include Team Members, VIPs, Customers, and Following, but you can edit these and add other circles to meet your needs. Plan a strategy for posting regularly and letting your customers know they can follow you on G+. I recommend posting an update at least once a week and including photos whenever possible.

Connecting Google+ to Your Website

After completing your profile and finding people to follow, add a Google+ button to your website so others can easily find and follow your business. To get the code, visit https://developers.google.com/+/plugins/badge/. Also add the Google+1 button to your website, so visitors to the page can +1 your site—the Facebook equivalent of liking it.

Interacting

Although it's great to have a profile and add a button to your website, the purpose of every social media network is to interact. Businesses can share updates, photos, videos, links, and events with the world or with specific circles. Each item of content created on the site is posted with a +1 button. This button allows others to, in essence, "like" your content and share it with others. Because reciprocity is key to effective social networking (and business success), businesses should use +1 to share content from others.

Pinterest

Pinterest (http://www.pinterest.com) is a virtual bulletin board that lets you share and organize images and videos linked to web pages on the Internet. Think of it as a scrapbook with "pages" of subject-specific content. The site's 11 million-plus members use their Pinterest boards to save and share decorating ideas, recipes, travel destinations, and other information. Pinterest is a great vehicle for businesses to share their product(s), information, and pictures relevant to their brands.

About Pinterest

- The biggest demographic for Pinterest is women ages 25 to 34.[26]
- Home décor is the most popular board category.[27]
- Pinterest users stay on the site for 15.8 minutes. (YouTube users stay on the site for an average of 16.4 minutes per visit, Facebook users stay for 12.1 minutes, and Twitter users a mere 3.3 seconds.[28])
- Pinterest is better than Facebook at reaching consumers: 70% of Pinterest users, compared with 17% of Facebook users, say they are on the respective sites for shopping inspiration.[29]

Creating an Account

To create a Pinterest account, request a login from a friend who already uses the site or from the site. After you receive an email invitation and accept it, you can create an account. The site will ask you to follow these steps:

- Link to either your Facebook or Twitter account.
- Create a user name.
- Choose an email address to associate with your account.
- Create a password.

Next, you'll need to verify your email. After your email has been verified, you can edit your Pinterest profile:

- Click your name in the upper right hand corner of the screen.
- Select **edit profile.**
- Change your notification settings.
- Make sure your first and last name or company name are correct.
- Complete the About Me section.
- Add your location.
- Add your website and other social media accounts.
- Change your profile picture.

Installing the Pin It Button

You may want to install a "Pin It" button to your browser's bookmark bar so you can easily pin images while browsing the web. Follow Pinterest's instructions for how to add the button to your specific browser, following relevant copyright law (*see* chapter 3).

Finding People to Follow

- Click **Find Friends** under your profile.
- Find and follow friends from Facebook, email, Gmail, and Yahoo.
- Invite friends who aren't on Pinterest.

Creating a Board

- Click Add + at the top right of your screen.
- Select **create a board.**
- Create a board name.
- Select a board category.
- Decide who can pin to your board (add a friend's name or invite them by email).
- Choose whether you want your board to be public or a secret board.
- Click **create.**

Secret Boards

Pinterest now allows users to create secret boards. Although these boards are private, users can invite friends to view them. Because this feature is still being tested, the number of secret boards allotted for each user is limited.

Secret boards offer individuals and businesses the chance to plan for events (surprise parties, gift ideas, company events, office redecorating, etc.) or other special occasions they may not want to share with others immediately, if ever. When pinning on these boards, none of the pins will show in your activity on Pinterest—not in the category sections, search results, or your home feeds. The boards will remain secret unless you decide to share them.

Secret boards are located at the bottom of the user profile page. When a user logs into Pinterest, a brief overview of this feature pops up for users who have not logged into Pinterest since the change was made. The help section also provides information about how to invite friends to a secret board and how to change the setting on a board from secret to public.

To go back to your board to make changes, select your profile drop-down menu and click **boards.** Click on the name of the board you want to edit. Select **edit board:**

- Edit the title.
- Add a description.
- Change the category.
- Change who can pin.

From the main boards page, you can select which pin you want to appear as the cover photo.

Uploading a Pin

- Click **Add +** on the top right of your page, and **upload pin.**
- Choose which board to pin the object to.
- Add a description of up to 500 words. Use keywords and give credit to the photo's creator.
- Click **edit.**
- Add a link for the site you would like the pin to go to.

Pinning a Photo from a Website

- Click the **Pin It** button on your bookmark bar.
- Choose a photo to pin.
- Select a board.
- Write a description and credit the photographer or source of the photo.
- Pin It.

Repinning within Pinterest

When you want to repin an object:

- Hover over the photo, and select **repin.**
- Choose the appropriate board.
- Modify the description and, again, ensure you give credit to the photographer.
- Pin It.

Branding with Pinterest

Construction Resources USA used Pinterest in a campaign to rebrand itself as CR Home Design—a total solution for home owners, remodelers, and designers. Although the previous company had an array of products and services available for do-it-yourselfers, it was viewed as a company for professional home builders and remodelers only. To refocus on the individual consumer, Construction Resources executives

- hired a person dedicated to marketing the company's new brand through Internet social sites;
- redesigned its website to be more user friendly, attractive, and functional for consumers;
- sought recognition for providing exemplary customer service; and

- promoted products with "glamour shots" of countertops, flooring, backsplashes, mirrors, and other desirable finishes.

Construction Resources also partnered with the Southern Coterie (a social network of blogs, recipes, photos, videos, events, and other content focused on Southern culture) with a contest to help spread brand awareness.

The "Entertaining with Southern Style" contest prompted followers to create a Pinterest board. Pinners had about a month to build their pin boards and tag their pins with #thesoutherncCONTEST. Pins included favorite southern tablescapes, country kitchens, welcoming front porches, cozy living spaces, and provincial entertaining pieces. The winner received a Big Green Egg (a highly coveted premium-quality ceramic charcoal outdoor smoker).

The Southern Coterie network and Construction Resources' blog, Facebook, Twitter, and Pinterest pages promoted the contest. More than 100 new followers joined Construction Resources' Pinterest page as a result of the contest and it created a library of shared content with hundreds of repins and likes. More important, the contest spread the company's influence as a source for interior design inspiration and helped in its transition from primarily a builder-focused business to one that is consumer focused and oriented toward home design.

Following the contest, the company has continued to add images to Pinterest and grow its influence among consumers.

Foursquare

Foursquare is a free mobile app that allows you to check in at businesses and other locations and share where you are with your friends. It can inspire new ideas about where to go and what to do because it offers personalized recommendations and deals based on what your friends and people like you have been doing. Business owners can use Foursquare to grow their companies because it helps them learn more about their customers and reach out to potential customers.

As of January 2013, more than 30 million people worldwide were using Foursquare, and the site had logged more than 3 billion check-ins.[30]

To get started with Foursquare, go to http://www.foursquare.com and download the mobile app to your iPhone, Android, or BlackBerry. Then create an account by signing up with Facebook or by email.

Claiming Your Venue

Before your business can get started with an account on Foursquare, you must first verify that you manage your location as follows:

- Sign into your Foursquare account.
- Visit the Foursquare for business website at http://www.foursquare.com/business.
- Select **venue owner.**
- Select **claim your venue.**
- Find your listing on Foursquare.
- Click **Do you manage this venue? Claim here.**
- Foursquare will verify by phone or email that you manage the business.

Merchant Dashboard

After Foursquare verifies you as a business owner, you can access useful information Foursquare compiles about your business, including:

- Total daily check-ins over time
- Most frequent visitors
- Most recent visitors
- Gender breakdown of each customer
- Time of day people check in

- Number of check-ins to your business that are broadcast to Facebook and Twitter

Use this information to tailor specials to customers who haven't visited recently or at all, to frequent loyal customers, and to those who haven't visited your business yet.

Creating a Special

Foursquare allows businesses to reward and attract customers with specials. The most common types of specials are

- a discount with a purchase ($10 off a $50 purchase);
- something for free (buy one, get a second one free);
- special treatment (behind the scenes tour at a museum or attraction); and
- reward for the best customers (get something free on your nth visit).

Keep your specials attractive by changing them regularly and offering multiple specials simultaneously. Promote them at your business and online through your website and email marketing. You can even promote checking in to access your specials via your Facebook and Twitter pages.

Instagram

Instagram, another free mobile app, allows you to manipulate your photos and share them with friends and family. Snap or upload a photo, choose from a variety of fun filters, post it to Instagram, and share it to Facebook, Twitter, or Tumblr. Instagram has more than 80 million users and businesses are pouncing on this creative and unique opportunity to share pictures of their products, fans, and more.

Getting Started with Instagram

- Go to http://www.instagram.com to download the mobile app onto your iPhone or Android device.
- Create an account by signing up with Facebook or by email.
- Import contacts and find friends from your contact list or Facebook.
- Follow suggested users.

Taking a Photo

- Select the **camera** or **share** tab along the bottom of the app.
- Select the **camera button** to take a new photo or the **gallery button** to choose from existing photos.
- View and select photo filters.
- Add a caption. Your caption can include hashtags (#topic) or tagging users (@user name). This will allow your photos to be visible to those searching for specific hashtags and group them together on Twitter if you post your photos to Twitter.
- Choose other social media outlets where you want to share your photo, such as Facebook, Twitter, Tumblr, email, Flickr, and Foursquare.
- Click **share.**

Feed Tab

The feed tab allows users to scroll through posts by all of the users you are following. You have the option to like or comment on photos as well as tweet them via your Twitter account. Businesses should follow their customers and encourage posting pictures of the company's products and tagging the company in these posts. Once a user shares a photo of your business or product(s), you should like it, comment on it, and share it on Twitter to demonstrate customer appreciation.

Popular Tab

The popular tab shows the most recently uploaded or popular photos from other users. Businesses can use this tab to find users who may be sharing photos relevant to the business or products.

News Tab

This tab quickly shows you when someone has liked or commented on your photos. It will also notify you when your Facebook friends join Instagram.

Profile Tab

The profile tab shows how many followers your account has and how many people you are following. You can also see all of your photos and photo map. Your photo map shows all of the geographic locations where you have taken photos, as long as you are tagging your photos with locations.

Houzz

Houzz is a collaborative platform for home building, re-modeling, and design. It convenes home owners and professionals in a visual community similar to Pinterest. Professionals can showcase projects and share their expertise by answering questions from users. They can also collaborate with clients using the site's Ideabooks.

Getting Started with Houzz

- Go to http://www.houzz.com.
- Enter an email address or connect with Facebook.
- Create a username and password.
- Select **home improvement professional / vendor.**

Filling Out Your Profile

Complete your profile with all of the following information so consumers can find and connect with you:

- Professional / firm name
- Category
- Website
- Contact details
- Business description
- Services provided
- Areas served

- Certification and awards
- Profile photo
- Link social media sites (Facebook, Twitter, Google+, Linkedin, blog/other)

Uploading Photos

When uploading a photo, you don't have to complete all fields, but the more you add, the more likely your business's photos are to appear in user search results. The options are as follows:

- Name
- Category (spaces or products)
- Style
- Metro area
- Project
- Price
- Link to website
- Description and photo credit

Projects

Projects allow builders to group categories of photos together in one place. For example, you might group your Houzz photos by different living spaces within the home or by community where the homes are located. Builders are able to create projects once they upload photos. Add the following information:

- Name
- City, state, and country
- Description
- Cover photo

Ideabooks

Are you working with a home buyer on their custom home design, remodeling, or decorating project? Houzz's Ideabooks allow businesses and home owners to save their visions, thoughts, and inspirations in one place where they can collaborate on projects.

Here's how to create your next Ideabook:

- Choose a title.
- Type a description and notes.
- Add your own or others' photos.
- Choose who you will collaborate with.

Other Houzz Features

Besides your own Ideabooks, look through home owners' books to observe new trends or products to incorporate into your projects, to search for professionals or vendors to work with on your next product, to read articles on the latest design and real estate trends, and to engage in discussions with other builders and home owners. Whatever you do, it's all about being social, building brand and, ultimately, enhancing your product!

Tumblr

Tumblr (http://www.tumblr.com) is a free blog platform where you can easily share photos, text, quotes, links, videos, and music. You name it; your business can share it. Almost 76 million blogs with more than 33 billion posts have been created on the site since its founding in 2007. One of the biggest benefits to creating a Tumblr account is that it can be accessed directly via the web, which means the search engines can index Tumblr content. Also, Tumblr posts can be integrated into your Facebook timeline, providing yet another way to create and share social media content.

Creating a Tumblr Account

- When you sign up, you'll be asked to designate a URL (www.businessname.tumblr.com).
- Tumblr will then ask you to choose your interests and it will show you blogs based on your choices.

Finally, you'll be given an opportunity to find contacts who might already be using Tumblr.

Customizing Your Tumblr Blog

Choose a theme and colors to match your company's branding. Tumblr allows for custom HTML layouts so you can have one designed to match your website or company blog.

Updating Settings

To guarantee you get the best return for your time on Tumblr, complete your profile, including the following:

- Avatar
- *Custom URL*
- A queue for content you create
- Sharing access for Facebook and Twitter
- An RSS feed

Click **allow search engines to index your blog.**

How and What to Post

Tumblr offers many options for posting fresh content that will attract attention. To maximize your visibility on Tumblr, create tags and a custom URL for each post.

- **Text.** Share content repurposed from your company blog or create original content. Tumblr also offers the options, for a fee, of pinning or highlighting your post.
- **Photo.** Post photos of a project or product, your team, customers using your product(s) or services, or company events and outings. You can even upload multiple photos to create a gallery.
- **Quote.** Has one of your employees said something particularly brilliant? Has an industry leader been quoted? Get their permission to share what they've said with the world!
- **Link.** Promote new features on your website. Link to industry-related news articles or blogs, or to other content relevant to your customers and business.
- **Chat.** Share humorous exchanges you've had with a client or customer or positive responses to your customer feedback survey. Just be sure to ask for the person's permission first.
- **Audio.** Post links to radio programs, songs related to your industry and links to your company's podcast or other industry-related podcasts.
- **Video.** Have a new ad or other cool promo video? Show it off!

Interacting with Others

Businesses shouldn't just be content creators; they should also be content amplifiers. Take a few minutes each time you log in to "like" or reply to Tumblr posts from those whom you are following and others. If you find something particularly appealing or inspirational, reblog it. (Get permission to do so from the original source and provide appropriate credit.)

Trulia

Trulia is a free real estate search engine with embedded social networking tools for consumers. Home builders, remodelers, and real estate agents can use it to interact with buyers. If you are an agent or broker, claim your listings on the site. Home builders, remodelers, and agents should take advantage of the site's free blog and Q&A section for home seekers. You can use the site to reach buyers directly and promote your homes and neighborhoods more broadly.

Creating your Profile

- Go to http://www.Trulia.com and click **Sign Up.**
- You can sign in with Facebook or complete the form and click **Create Account.**

- Upload your profile photo (a head-and-shoulders photo that looks professional).
- Describe yourself in the headline using 75 characters (e.g., Jacksonville New Homes Specialist).
- Add your phone number.
- Set the URL for your public profile (e.g., http://www.Trulia.com/profile/carolflammer/).
- Add your website URL, blog, and links to your other social media sites.
- Complete the sections on Experience, About Me, and Testimonials.

In the Experience section you may want to list your past two to three positions or detail your credentials. Under About Me, discuss your specialties and provide some insight into your personality. Then, ask clients or customers to add testimonials to your page. If you already have testimonials that you have permission to use online, add them.

Claim your Listings

After creating your user profile, claim your listings. Click **My Listings** (you must be logged in) and find listings by property address, MLS ID, or email address. After you claim listings, you can edit them and see how many times people have viewed them. Listings are claimed on a "first-come, first-served" basis. The agent (or other profile user) that claims first gets his or her contact information on the listing, so make sure you get to your listings before other agents do.

Blogging on Trulia

You can post blogs and link to your website and custom blog free of charge on Trulia. It is simple to use, so it can be a great place to start blogging and building a following while your own blog is under construction. You can create referring links by using keywords and anchor text. Follow these steps:

- Click **Write New Post** to start a new post.
- Add a title (informative, catchy, and brief). Titles need to capture readers' attention. Consider the newspaper headlines or evening news promotions that entice you to watch. My post titled "Where's My Homebuyer Tax Credit?" attracted 106 views without any promotion.
- Select a category.
- Add your location.
- Type your content, a 250–350-word, conversational blog entry. Although you can cut and paste text, you must do it from a plain text program like Notepad that will not add unnecessary coding.

Figure 4.6 Blog on Trulia

Blogging on Trulia will promote your homes and communities to more consumers. (Source: Reprinted with permission from Trulia)

- Include a link or two in your text. Highlight the anchor text and click the **link icon** on the toolbar (fig. 4.6).
- Copy and paste the URL of the website or page you are linking to.
- Enter a description of the website or page.
- Add at least one photo, sized appropriately for the web (72 *dpi* = medium resolution). Click the

photo box in the toolbar and browse your computer or the Internet for the image. You can click **more options** to specify where in the post you want the image to appear. You can also enter an image description.

- Click **done.**
- Click **publish.**
- Review and edit your blog entry.

Q&A with Potential Buyers

You can establish expertise in a niche and create relationships with potential home buyers by answering questions on Trulia. Buyers ask questions on topics from how to repair their credit to how to buy a foreclosed property.

- Click **Q&A** in the My Trulia box at the upper right area of the page.
- Click the **Trulia Voices** link in the middle of the page.
- Click **View Most Recent Questions.**
- To answer a question, click it. Then click, **Answer This Question** and type your answer.
- To ask a question, type it in the text box in the Ask a Question box.

ActiveRain

With more than 320,000 members, ActiveRain (http://
www.activerain.com) promotes itself as the largest and
most active professional social network and marketing
platform in the real estate industry. The ActiveRain Real
Estate Network is free and provides opportunities for
home builders, remodelers, real estate agents, and others
in the real estate community to interact.

A basic profile is free, but becoming a Rainmaker
offers exposure outside the ActiveRain network to
search engines and to more than 2 million visitors who
come to the site in a month. Rainmakers also can access
training from leading experts in the housing industry.
ActiveRain can be a great way to add another result to
your page one SERP results and interact with co-op
agents who can help sell your homes.

Creating an Account

Select **Sign Up** on the upper right corner of the home
page and follow the directions. As with YouTube, your
user name will be part of your URL on ActiveRain. For
example, if your user name is MitchLevinson, your profile URL will be http://ActiveRain.com/mitchlevinson.

You will receive a confirmation email message with a link. When you click it, you can update your profile as follows:

- Upload a profile photo or company logo.
- Explain who you are and your specialty in the About Me section.
- Complete your profile with pertinent information that makes you stand out. You can customize and rename sections to make them more applicable to your company. You can add links to your website, Facebook page, Twitter profile, blog, and other sites. Atlanta Realtor Jim Crawford (http://activerain.com/xavier) with RE/MAX Paramount Properties has customized his page with buttons that click through to his website, his biography and a robust section of client testimonials.

After you are satisfied with your profile, start looking for associates (the equivalent of Facebook friends). You can also join groups of other real estate professionals within specific niches of the real estate industry and ActiveRain.

ActiveRain also gives you a personal blog and the capability to send your blog posts to Localism.com (a consumer portal), your group members, categories, and other ActiveRain channels.

Using the Blog

Click **Write a Blog Post** at the top of the page to start a new post.

- Type a title.
- Type your entry or cut and paste it from a text editor like Notepad.
- Add a link or two to your text: highlight the word or words to link to and click the **link icon** on the toolbar.
- Enter the entire site address.
- Leave target as "Open link in a new window."
- Title the link.
- Select three to four relevant tags. (Include these words in your blog post.)
- Add photos. Click the box with the **tree** in the toolbar. If you click the box to the right of the image URL you can upload from your computer instead of entering a URL. Enter an image description and a title and use the appearance tab to specify where in the post the image will appear. Click **insert.**
- Select the channels, groups, and categories you wish to post to.
- Publish, review, and edit your entry as necessary.

Finding Associates

- Click **Search** at the top right of the page.
- Type keywords (e.g., "St. Paul," "golf communities").
- To narrow the search results to individuals only, click **members** at the top of the page.
- When you see a member you think you want to connect with, click his or her link and view the profile.
- From the profile, click **Add as Associate** under the profile picture and add the person to a group.

You can also add notes that will be visible to anyone viewing the associates on your profile.

Joining Groups

- Click **Groups** at the top right of the page, next to Search.
- Search for groups (use the drop-down box under Browse Groups or type a keyword in the text box under Search Groups and click **Search**).
- To join, click the group's link.
- On the left of the group page, click **Join Group.**

You can share your blog posts with a group by selecting it from the drop-down menu on your blog. If you want to post a blog entry only to the group's profile, go to that group and click **Post to Group** at the top left of the page. Type your blog post as you normally would. This will publish your entry only in the group, not on your personal blog.

RealtyJoin

RealtyJoin (http://www.RealtyJoin.com) is a social networking site designed to help real estate investors, service providers, home builders, remodelers, and other professionals find opportunities and establish connections. RealtyJoin users can create enhanced profiles. Each user has a personal WordPress blog on the site. The site also has options for loading videos, photos, seeking project bids online, and social networking.

Creating an Account

- Register directly through the home page.
- Select a user name, enter your email address, and create a password.
- The next screen allows you to invite your contacts and friends.
- Create an account by completing all profile details (this is what site visitors see): Type your first and

last name—for example, Carol Morgan—in the profile details. Other fields include Company Name, Primary Specialty, and About Me.

- After you have joined the site, you can log in by entering your user name and password at the top right area of the page.
- If your profile photo does not automatically display, you can go to the Edit Profile section and update your avatar by uploading an image directly to RealtyJoin. You can also go to Gravatar (http: //www.gravatar.com) and get a globally recognized avatar. Your Gravatar is associated with your email address so wherever you log in with that address your Gravatar will display.
- Click **Member Dashboard** at the top left of page. You will see a personal dashboard with friend requests, group activity, and messages. You can edit your profile there.
- Add a logo to your profile. The site will automatically resize your logo to fit.

RealtyJoin also gives you a personal WordPress blog but you must set it up. Click the **Express Yourself: Start Your Own RealtyJoin Blog** button on the left side of your profile page.

Create your blog as follows:

- **Name your blog.** The name will display in the masthead at the top of your blog, so use proper capitalization and spaces between words.
- **Create your blog's URL,** for example, http:// realtyjoin.com/carolmorgan.
- **Choose the desired privacy level.** There are two options. I recommend the first one, which is to allow your blog to be visible in the search engines. The second option will only display your blog posts to others on the RealtyJoin site.

Using the Blog

You can customize the blog header with your own branded art. Consider including your logo and tagline.

Edit the About page. Write a short autobiography or an overview of your blog and what you plan to write about. This will help readers determine whether they want to follow you. When you are ready to blog, go to the Dashboard and click **Add New** from the Posts drop-down menu on the left side of the dashboard.

You can use HTML code or the Visual Editor.

- Type the title of your post under Add New Post.
- Type your entry or cut and paste it from a text editor like Notepad.

- Add a link or two to your text by highlighting the word or words you want to link to. Click the **link icon** on the toolbar.
- Enter the link address.
- Leave target as "Open link in a new window."
- Title the link.
- Type three to four relevant tags. These words also should be included in your blog entry.
- Select a category for your post. You may want to add all the blog categories the first time you post, so you do not have to continually add them. Think about the topics you plan to write and brainstorm the categories for your blog based on your content.
- Add photos. Click the box to the right of **upload / insert.** If you have trouble uploading, you may want to select the **browser uploader** option. There are also options to upload from a URL or a media library.
- Preview your entry, edit it, and click **Publish** to post it.

Connecting with RealtyJoin Members

RealtyJoin offers many options for connecting with others:

- Use the search box on the member directory pages to search for a specific member by name, company name, or business type.
- Click **Member Directory** from the top navigation to review RealtyJoin members and select those you want to connect with for business.
- Click the **Invite Anyone** option in the left sidebar to invite other contacts to the site.

Joining Groups

Click **Groups** in the top navigation. You can review groups and choose an existing group to join. You can start your own group by selecting "create a group."

Linkedin

Linkedin is an online Rolodex and résumé. Use it to

- build connections;
- establish expertise by asking and answering questions;
- get recommendations; and
- post jobs and events.

Linkedin is a great tool for building personal brand. You can create a page for your business as well. The search engines index both personal and business pages.

After building your Linkedin account, promote it via your website, blog, email signature, Facebook page, and your other sites.

Linkedin helps you maintain contact with people no matter how many times they change jobs. I use it as a mini *customer relationship management* (*CRM*) system for my connections. Linkedin allows me to keep up with people that I don't need to email every day so I don't overwhelm my Outlook contacts database. I try to invite everyone I meet to connect with me via Linkedin, so I can reach out to them when the right opportunity arises.

Creating an Account

Think executive bio when you create your public profile. Enter the following information:

- Name (women might want to include their maiden names)
- Previous employers or companies (former associates may not know where you are now)
- Photo
- Education
- Contact information (phone number and email address)
- URL (your website, blog, other sites)

● Twitter (add your Twitter account, but don't set it to post everything you tweet to your Linkedin account)

Customize your public profile's URL and choose what to include in your public profile.

You can enhance your professional profile by clicking on the Improve your profile button on your profile page. It will prompt you to include more about your education, details of past jobs, languages, projects, and courses.

Making Connections

Connect with people as follows:

● Send a personal note with your invitation to connect.
● Connect with colleagues. Linkedin can search your email for connections or you can find possible connections using Linkedin's search function.
● Clean out that drawer or box of business cards you have and add those contacts to Linkedin. You can finally throw the cards away!
● Add new acquaintances to your Linkedin account.

- Ask your connections to introduce you to their connections on Linkedin using the Get Introduced function.

Having many connections increases the likelihood that people will see your profile first, even if they're searching for someone else.

Managing Your Connections

You can manage your connections by making notes on your connections profiles (these notes are only visible to you). If you need to find a person whose name you can't remember, you can sort contacts by state or industry. If you need more robust management tools, consider upgrading to a paid account.

Recommendations

Request recommendations from your best customers and provide recommendations for your vendors. Providing recommendations positions your name on the person's page you are recommending and increases your visibility. For example, if you love this book, please go to my Linkedin profile (http://www.Linkedin.com/in/carolmorganflammer) and add a recommendation. You can do the same for your attorney, accountant, business coach, and others you work with. If you like their work, tell them, and tell other people about them.

Endorsements

One of the most useful features of Linkedin is a new endorsements section. Endorsements allow professionals to easily validate the skills and expertise peers have added to their profiles. It's a quick alternative to a recommendation that allows you to tell the Linkedin world the skills your connection has. You will see all of your connection's endorsements in the Skills & Expertise section on their page.

Here's how to endorse your connections:

- At the top of a connection's profile, you'll see recommended endorsements. Simply click on the skills you want to endorse them for.
- You can suggest skills.

When a connection endorses you, Linkedin will notify you by email and on your personal profile. You can see who has endorsed you by visiting your own Skills & Expertise section. You can accept new skills your colleagues recommend and add skills.

FAQs on Endorsement Etiquette

Q. What if someone endorses me, but I don't want others to see the endorsement?

A. Click their face next to the skill they have endorsed you for. Select **hide endorsement.**

Q. If someone endorses me, do I have to endorse them?

A. Endorsing someone doesn't take much time, and it's always good to return positive favors!

Q. Is endorsing someone worth my time?

A. Don't go on an endorsing spree, but if your peer has performed exceptionally well at something or if you know they are looking for a new job in a specific field, you could help them by endorsing them.

Create a Company Profile

Linkedin company profiles display the date the company was founded, a corporate biography, number of employees, and their average age. Clients and associates can review your company's profile for background and corporate culture information prior to business meetings. Also add the following:

- Company name
- Logo

- Biography
- Specialties
- Related companies
- Your blog

Make sure your employees list your company name correctly on their profiles so they will appear on Linkedin's roster for your company.

You can enhance your company profile with an expanded products and services section. For example, go online to http://tinyurl.com/d94c6s and click the services tab. Provide details about specific products or services your company offers and an image, video, description, special promotion, and the person to contact for more information.

Posting and Finding Jobs

The Jobs section allows you to post available positions and research job opportunities. The Find Jobs section automatically populates with jobs matching your current job description. You also can search for jobs by job title, keywords, or company name. Posting a job is easy, but not free.

Groups

Position yourself as an expert by joining or starting groups on Linkedin and becoming a connector. Groups are a great way to field questions, share news stories, and interact with others. The number of groups on Linkedin can be overwhelming, so start with groups you already belong to *IRL*. I am a member of the Atlanta Green Communicators, my local Chamber of Commerce, a local newspaper's group, the Georgia Chapter of the Public Relations Society of America and a women's networking group. There is even a group for entrepreneurs called On Startups. These online groups allow you to sustain and extend your relationships with members beyond monthly or quarterly meetings. Linkedin also suggests groups you may like based on your profile. Click on the Groups tab to see "Groups you may like." Visit some of them to see if you want to participate.

Linkedin Do's

- Secure your URL.
- Complete your entire profile.
- Update your status weekly.
- Join groups.

- Write recommendations.
- Create a corporate profile.
- Answer questions—the more you give the more you get back.

Linkedin Don'ts

- Feel pressured to give an introduction or recommendation.
- Forward questionable requests to your connections.
- Become spam by inviting everyone you remotely know to connect.
- Forget to update your status at least once a month.

Why to Use Linkedin

- Increase your visibility and build personal brand.
- Make connections and build a better network.
- Improve your Google results.
- Perform reference checks on individuals and companies.
- Gauge the health of a company.
- Ask for advice.
- Offer advice and establish your expertise.

Tying it Together With Online Apps

Linkedin offers a number of applications to tie your social media sites together. Review them and incorporate some into your profile.

- **Blog (WordPress or TypePad).** Incorporate your WordPress or TypePad blog into your Linkedin personal profile.
- **Company Buzz.** Add tweets about your company or other key search terms to your profile.
- **SlideShare and Google Presentation.** Make your latest presentations available online.
- **Box.net.** Share and collaborate on an array of file types.
- **My Travel.** Allow others to see your travel schedule using TripIt.
- **Reading List by Amazon.** Share what you are reading with others.
- **Polls.** Find out what your connections think about a specific topic by adding a poll to your profile.
- **Huddle Workspaces.** Collaborate on a project with others in a private workspace.

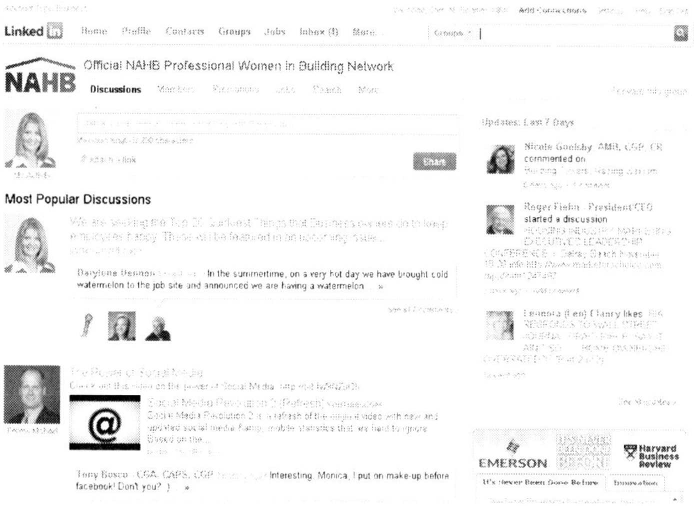

Figure 4.7 **Professional Women in Building Linkedin group page**

Professional women in building stay connected and share ideas through a Linkedin group. (Source: National Association of Home Builders)

Joining Groups Keeps Those Far Away Closer

The NAHB's Professional Women in Building Network has a group on Linkedin (fig. 4.7). We use it to keep in touch with one another between board meetings and to promote the council's events. We have discussed best practices for social media and how to motivate staff during tough economic times.

A recent post promoted a scholarship awards webinar and explained how to participate in the awards. Group members have used the Get Introduced feature to create a warm handshake in today's competitive business environment.

Photo Sharing Sites

A study by BHI Media on home elevations revealed that color renderings or photos on home listings and on the builder's website increased the number of home shoppers who click for more details by 30%.[31] On the other hand, a line drawing, black and white photo, or no image decreased clicks by 30%. Take advantage of the web to show off your homes and communities in full color.

Flickr

Flickr allows users to load and share galleries of photos along with their profiles. Because Yahoo owns Flickr, it ranks high in a Yahoo image search. Posting photos on Flickr increases the likelihood they will appear in the results when users enter your keywords in their photo searches. Pictures are a valuable marketing asset; make sure yours look professional. Also, don't use captions and descriptions to try to sell products; Flickr is for non-commercial use. Instead, you can add appropriate tags and titles to help search engines locate your photos. Rather than naming your photo "Chestnut Crossing," consider labeling it with more keywords such as "Chestnut Crossing Single Family Homes [Name of Builder] Georgetown KY 38888." You could include even more descriptors, such as three-bedroom home, energy efficient, or anything else home buyers might be looking for that your community has. Remodelers should post before and after photos of kitchen, master bedroom, and bathroom projects with keywords that home owners might use when searching for a remodeling company.

Creating a Flickr Account

Go to http://www.yahoo.com and click **Sign Up** to get a Yahoo ID if you don't already have one. (This ID will allow you to create a My Yahoo page and use tools in addition to Flickr, such as Yahoo instant messaging and Yahoo Mail.) Then click **Sign Up to create your account** at http://www.flickr.com and enter your Yahoo ID. You could instead sign in using your Facebook or Google ID.

Personalize your profile.

- Create your "buddy icon" by uploading your logo or photo.
- Choose your customized Flickr URL (your company name or your name depending on whether

the page is for personal or business use. Mine is http://www.flickr.com/photos/mrelevance).

- Personalize your profile with your name, time zone, gender, and description. (If you are creating a business profile, just add the time zone and description.)
- Upload photos.
- Add tags (keywords) and descriptions.
- Create sets (photo groupings). You may want to create a set of photos for a specific community or group photos by floor plan or room type.
- Find friends on Flickr. Search an existing address book on Yahoo, Gmail, or Windows live.
- Search for people by name. You can add a person to your account as a contact, a friend, or a family member.
- Join groups. Find groups on Flickr that match your interests. Groups exist for green building, condos, home and garden, and other industry specialties.

Photo sharing websites add another dimension to your social networking on Facebook and Twitter and enable you to post photos easily to your blog and on other sites. As with YouTube, a photo sharing site can help you show images of a home under construction to clients without having them go to the jobsite. Atlanta based CR Home uses Flickr to post images on a rotating photo gallery on its website (http://crhomeusa.com/). The images include event shots with groups of people, as well as product shots. You can visit the Flickr page at http://www.flickr.com/photos/constructionresources.

Making a Visual Impression

Decatur, Georgia, kitchen and bath supplier Construction Resources Inc. uses Flickr to display its installed products in finished installations (fig. 4.8). It has been a great way to reach out to consumers, architects and designers.

"We showcase our products as well as our events on the site," said Mitch Hires, president of Construction Resources. "This provides a very compelling visual example of our available products and our finished work. Because home owners have a hard time visualizing what the final installation of their countertop or other products might look like, our photos on Flickr give them an opportunity to visualize the possibilities."

Klout

Klout is an online tool for measuring and leveraging your social media influence. It is a great tool for busi-

Figure 4.8 **A Flickr page**

A robust photo gallery can help buyers visualize your products. (Source: Reprinted with permission from Construction Resources, Decatur, Georgia)

nesses to enhance their credibility with buyers. Klout measures influence online using data generated from social networks. Higher scores reflect higher levels of engagement. In addition, users can give +Ks to people they follow to indicate expertise. For instance, I'm considered to be an expert on social media, public relations, and Atlanta. Your expertise could be food, pets, travel, "green," or golf.

Currently, Klout scores everyone who has a social media presence even if they don't have a Klout profile. By joining the site, you will connect your profiles together in Klout, allowing you to better manage your score.

Recent Klout updates enhanced the capabilities of the influence meter. The site now measures more than 400 social media signals from 12 billion data points across multiple social media platforms including Facebook, Twitter, Google+, Linkedin, Foursquare, YouTube, Instagram, Tumblr, Blogger, WordPress.com, Last.fm, and Flickr. The site also has integrated Wikipedia into its inputs to better measure influence both online and offline and has adjusted the distribution of scores to reflect the boom in engagement across the Internet. Although these updates are important for your overall score, the newest tool, "Your Moments," is probably the most useful for a typical user. Your Moments displays your recent content and ideas that have been the most influential across all of your social networks. It also shows patterns of interaction so you can see the information your followers find most useful.

Ultimately, Klout is all about proving to your buyers that you are relevant and important in your field. It also dramatically improves your relevance and engagement across social media platforms by showing you what people want.

As a consumer, what I like most about Klout is the metric it provides to companies for prioritizing customer service. Yes, that's right: if you have a high Klout score—

typically above 50—companies will respond to you more quickly than to people with a lower Klout score. So, if you post a comment on social media about a problem with your laptop, airline reservation, a restaurant meal, or another product, service, or experience, you may have the issue resolved more quickly if you have a higher Klout score. For companies overwhelmed with customer complaints, by all means look at your product, service, and customer experience, but also use Klout scores as one tool to allocate customer service resources.

And then there are perks. We all like those, right? Well, for those of us with high Klout scores (mine is typically 68–70), companies offer freebies. I received a wine gift from Bing and a four-pack of Red Bull. Others have gotten gifts such as a Nike Fuel Band.

Other Internet Tools

The Internet offers hundreds if not thousands of other social networking sites, coupon sites, and tools:

- **Craigslist** (http://www.craigslist.org) advertises jobs, housing, items for sale, personals, events, and more, for free. Consider listing homes, announcing events, and posting press releases there. Builders and agents have reported great traffic from this site.

- **Squidoo** (http://www.squidoo.com) allows users to create free web pages (called lenses) on particular topics or subjects. Consider launching a lens about your company and joining related groups.

- **Ning** (http://www.ning.com) allows users to create their own social networks around specific subject matter. Because great groups on homes and real estate already exist, you don't need to create your own. Just join and participate in an existing Ning group for your target market.

- **Yelp** (http://www.yelp.com) allows users to write reviews and recommendations of businesses including restaurants, stores, and nightclubs. Ask happy customers to contribute a positive review of your company here.

- **Social bookmarking sites** enable users to share and manage articles and favorite websites. Yahoo Buzz, DIGG, Delicious, Propeller, Reddit, Sphinn, and Stumbleupon are some of my favorite bookmarking sites. By bookmarking content and adding tags, you can find web pages and websites easily in the future. For instance, I bookmarked the statistics I needed for this book in my Delicious account (http://www.delicious.com/carolmflammer) and then tagged them "social media" and "statistics" or "women" and "statistics." Later, I could sort by one of those tags to find all of the content related to that topic.

Text Messaging

Sixty-eight percent of cell phone users regularly send text messages.[32] According to a survey conducted for Placecast by Harris Interactive, many mobile users would like to receive alerts and information on their cell phones from places they frequent.[33] A recent Harris Interactive survey found that 42% of 18–34-year-olds and 33% of 35–44-year-olds with cell phones were interested in receiving alerts on their cell phones from places they frequent.[34]

Text messaging can provide your buyers with instant gratification. When you include texting options on signs and ads, buyers can text you for information on your neighborhood, listing, or upcoming event.

Quick Response (QR) Codes

A quick response (QR) code is a two-dimensional bar code you scan using a smartphone with a QR code reader. It enables quick access to websites that display information contained in the QR code. QR codes have several advantages: They can hold hundreds of times more information than traditional bar codes; they are readable from any direction; and even if they are slightly damaged or obscured, they are still readable. Real estate agents are using QR codes on signs and flyers to provide buyers with information, including videos of homes.

Build Systematically

Don't be overwhelmed by all the possible tools in your social media toolbox. Remember to start your SMM program with your blog as the hub. It will serve as the foundation of your entire program and can feed information to other social networking sites. Plan your program strategically to use the social networking sites that make the most sense to reach your target audiences. Smaller companies may want to choose to just use a blog and one or two social networking sites, whereas larger ones may want to launch and utilize most of the sites mentioned in this chapter. Social media is not one-size-fits-all. Just as a sub maker personalizes a sandwich for a unique customer, you can create a social media experience to entice consumers with the right ingredients.

Online Public Relations

An online public relations strategy augments your traditional PR program. Instead of interacting with the public through traditional media and events, online PR provides an avenue not only for SEO, but also to reach multiple target audiences directly, including members of the media. A study by Brunswick Research found that more than two-thirds of journalists have written a story about something they found through social media.[35] The study focused on trends in the use of social media by global business journalists. Following are the study's key findings:

- Social media is an increasingly influential source of information for journalists.
- Social media has a positive effect on the quality of journalism, including the angle and content of stories.
- Nine out of 10 journalists have used social media to investigate an issue.

- Twitter provides the most valuable information sources but blogs often provide a foundation for a story.
- North American journalists use and believe in social media more than journalists in other locations do.
- 72% of journalists said social media will play an increasing role in their profession.
- 25% get information from online public relations distribution services, other online subscriptions, and Google Alerts.

A Middleberg / Ross study[36] found that 98% of journalists go online daily searching for news:

- 92% research articles on the web.
- 76% look for new expert sources on the web.
- 73% use the Internet to find press releases.

Online PR allows you to control your messages. By incorporating keywords, anchor text, and links in your online news releases, you transform them into a powerful SMO tool. Google "Gerstad Builders" to see how one builder has filled its search results with a combination of blogs, online PR, and its own website.

Another recent poll found that 89% of journalists depend on social media for story research:[37]

- 89% use blogs for story research.
- 65% use social networking sites.
- 52% use microblogging sites like Twitter.
- 61% use information from Wikipedia.

One major concern journalists expressed was that the information on social media sites is often unreliable. Because online media greatly influence traditional media, businesses can extend their reach by using online channels. By posting stories online, you can become the expert source journalists discover in their Internet searches. Press releases will contribute positively to your SEO because you can place links to your website in them. Many sites designed to distribute online press releases allow keyword anchor text as well. Both paid and free websites allow businesses to post online press releases (*see* Resources). Shop these companies to determine which will suit your needs. Some will display releases online and email them to reporters. PRWeb.com (fig. 5.1) and http://www.pitchengine.com are great options for the budget conscious. Choose services that allow you to incorporate links and anchor text in your press releases.

Figure 5.1 **PRWeb.com**

PRWeb is one of many online press release distribution services. (Source: Reprinted with permission from Isakson Living, Norcross, Georgia)

Top Three Ways to Distribute Content

You have timely, newsworthy information about your newest community, product, sales successes, or home plans. How do you distribute it? You can use two traditional methods of verbally pitching your story to the media or emailing a press release. You can also use a third option—social media—to get the word out.

1. **Pitching.** Pitching is still a very effective way to get a major media outlet to cover your story. Often newspapers and other media don't want to compete with one another for stories. By pitching the story as an exclusive to just one reporter you have the opportunity for more in-depth coverage of your story. Once the story runs in the first publication you can release it to other publications and post it online. The key to pitching and scoring is to understand the reporter you are pitching to. Avoid calling reporters when they are on deadline and understand their publications and the types of stories they will cover. Don't throw a reporter a curve ball with an irrelevant pitch. Reserve your capital with reporters for major news. Your new community with 50 deposits for homes that are not yet built is worth pitching.

2. **Press Releases.** A PR staple, the press release is still a crucial part of telling your story to the media.

Press releases are an excellent way to reach many news outlets simultaneously. We usually send press releases for features, rather than news stories. The grand opening of your new community, a new product, or a new floor plan is suitable material for a press release.

3. **Social Media.** This is the newest venue for distributing content. It's fast (you can reach millions of people with a single mouse click), and it places your company news in the venue that most people are using. From online press releases to blogging, social media provides an instant platform for your information. Plus, you can incorporate SEO to break through the noise and launch your content to the top of the news agenda.

How to Write a Press Release

Place contact information (name, telephone number, email address) at the top of the page. The headline clearly states the subject of the release and is usually centered in bold type. Include the location of the news in a *dateline* preceding the text of the news release. The first paragraph should catch the reader's attention and answer "who?" "what?" "where?" "when?" "why?" and "how?". It should contain a news peg, telling the readers why they should care about the topic right now.

The second and third paragraphs should provide more details and at least one quote from a person relevant to the news story. When you quote this source, use his or her full name with a complete identification, including a title or position, and company. Quotes allow you to add a positive endorsement to a press release. For example, if your model home just won an award, you may refer to the award and use phrases such as "award-winning community" in your press release and then describe the classic architecture or modern decor. However, if you want to include opinion in the release, such as a statement that the home is "beautiful" or "outstanding" or "the best value," you'll need to put that in quotes and attribute it to a credible source.

Boilerplate text that describes your company, similar to an *elevator speech,* should follow the news story. Include your website's and social media site's URLs. This text should be part of your press release template because you will only update it as needed, rather than creating a new "speech" for every release.

Figure 5.2 shows a press release in the proper format.

After your press release is written, review your list of keywords and incorporate a few of them into the release. Use them on sites that allow anchor text to link to your website or your blog. Most marketers who are not versed in it overlook this method of SEO.

RealtyJoin®

CONTACT INFORMATION

RELEASE DATE:
March 8, 2011

CONTACT:
mRELEVANCE
Carol Flammer: 770-383-3360 x20
Carol@mRELEVANCE.com

HEADLINE

RealtyJoin Launches Version 2.0 · An Enhanced Social Marketplace

DATELINE

ATLANTA – RealtyJoin, a free interactive social and business networking site for the real estate industry in the United States and Canada, announces the launch of version 2.0. This totally redesigned real estate social networking site does everything that the original version of RealtyJoin did, only better. The new, enhanced RealtyJoin website is a social marketplace for the entire real estate industry where individuals can connect, network and advertise potential opportunities.

RealtyJoin 2.0 offers a more user-friendly integrated website that includes WordPress blogs for all users, upgraded navigation, enhanced profiles, video options, upcoming events, the ability to post status updates, photos and video.

QUOTES

We decided to start RealtyJoin because we saw that real estate investors, REALTORS®, tradespeople, home builders and designers were looking for good, Internet-based tools to help them network, find and advertise opportunities, said Andy Heller, a veteran real estate investor and public speaker, as well as RealtyJoin co-founder. "Our site is a community for real estate agents, investors, plumbers and electricians, stagers, home builders and anyone who believes that the free exchange of information will increase sales."

Ilyce Glink, an award-winning, nationally syndicated columnist, blogger, bestselling author and radio talk show host recently joined the RealtyJoin team to oversee content strategy. Glink says she has been impressed with RealtyJoin's ability to connect individuals and offer them the ability to share pertinent industry related content.

"In just a few short months, RealtyJoin proved there is a real need for a place where real estate investors and the companies they work with can connect and share information," she said. A number of high profile real estate groups and associations are participating in RealtyJoin, including the Atlanta Board of Realtors®, Foreclosure.com, Southeast Valley Regional Association of Realtors®, and RIS Media.

RealtyJoin offers the real estate industry an opportunity to gain business traction by starting online conversations and relationship with buyers, sellers, architects, contractors, brokers, suppliers and other professionals.

BOILERPLATE TEXT

The introductory level of RealtyJoin remains free. Premium and executive memberships will be available over the next several months for those seeking further upgrades and enhancements.

For more information on RealtyJoin 2.0 and to join the premiere social marketplace of the real estate industry, visit www.RealtyJoin.com. "Like" RealtyJoin on Facebook at www.facebook.com / RealtyJoin and follow RealtyJoin on Twitter at http://twitter.com/RealtyJoin

\# \# \#

Figure 5.2 **Press release**

A press release includes contact information, a bold headline, a dateline, keywords, and your elevator speech.

When you are submitting press releases directly to media outlets, you should only distribute information that is truly newsworthy. If you constantly send press releases to the media that they do not deem newsworthy, reporters and editors will ignore your email messages. On the other hand, although reporters may not find your latest sales incentive newsworthy (considering it advertising, rather than news), online consumers probably will. Go ahead and write it up for online distribution. Even if it isn't breaking news, you can still post it on a variety of online sites and distribute it through news distributors like those mentioned in the section below. In addition, don't assume that all stories must be time sensitive. Many builders have lifestyle or feature stories without an immediate expiration date that are perfect for online distribution. However, ensure that these evergreen stories capture readers' attention and motivate them to keep reading by showing how the story is important or useful.

Post press releases to your website's press room as they are released. This online newsroom should be easily accessible from your home page. Consider adding it to the main navigation as a "News" tab or as part of the drop-down menu under "About." Your online newsroom should contain a corporate backgrounder, corporate fact sheet, or both; recent press releases; and your corporate logo (*see* http://www.wilsonparkerhomes. com/atlanta-new-homes/press-room.php).

Press releases should display in reverse chronological order so reporters and consumers can easily find the most recent news. If you have videos you want to make available to reporters, add those to your newsroom as well.

If uploading releases to your main website is cumbersome, consider adding a press section to your blog and uploading them there instead.

As company press releases accumulate online, Google your name. You will probably like what you see!

News Distributors

PRnewswire.com and BusinessWire.com are the oldest and most established sites in online public relations. They had established relationships with media outlets long before social media was invented. Both do an excellent job of targeting reporters and populating the Internet with a number of stories within an hour or so of release. Their per-release fees vary depending on the number of words, media lists targeted, and whether a photo is included and/or archived. The Daybook service, available in Atlanta, Dallas, and Nashville, also has delivered consistently positive results. NHDbuzz.com (fig. 5.3), a subsidiary of New Homes Directory, places

Figure 5.3 NHD Buzz

You can post online news stories for free at NHD Buzz. (Source: Reprinted with permission from NHD Buzz, Murrieta, California)

press releases at no cost as a service to the new home industry. The site also features a Q&A section, "Ask Carol," where you can get answers to public relations and social media questions (fig. 5.4).

Becoming an Expert Source

In addition to populating keyword search results with press releases demonstrating your company's expertise, you can also take advantage of a free online service to review and respond to reporter queries. Help a Reporter Out (HARO) was started in 2008 by entrepreneur and social media guru Peter Shankman. Almost 30,000 reporters from local, regional, national and international media outlets (*Huffington Post, USA Today, New York Times*, television news shows, Internet outlets, and others) post queries related to stories they are researching, and subscribing sources respond when they can help. Each weekday, subscribers receive several emails with queries organized by general topic areas, including business, healthcare, real estate, and lifestyle. Many subscribing sources also follow HARO on Twitter and Facebook to receive up-to-the-minute queries.

To become a subscribing source, visit http://helpareporter.com. When you sign up, you will agree to respond to queries only when you have relevant information, and you will agree not to contact any re-

ASK CAROL

NHD Buzz   New Homes   Builders   Real Estate   Green Homes

Ask Carol

Best Time to Pitch a Story

Top Three Ways to Distribute Content

What Results Should I Expect From Social Media Marketing?

Are Home Builders Still Hosting Events?

What are the Twitter Do's and Don'ts for Home Builders?

What Is Ask Carol - Make Sense Of All The Latest Internet Buzz

Jump to page 1
Total articles found 6

Figure 5.4 "Ask Carol" Q&A

Ask Carol answers questions about PR and Social Media. (Source: Reprinted with permission from NHD Buzz, Murrieta, California)

porter you find on HARO with unrelated news. That means you may not add the reporter to an email list without permission (the list's strict adherence to privacy policies is one thing that attracts reporters and keeps them coming back).

When you find a query you can answer, simply follow the instructions to respond. You will have the most success when you offer succinct information. The reporter will follow up with questions if needed (don't be surprised if you don't get a response).

HARO queries often include deadlines, and it's vital to adhere to them. If the query generates too many responses for the reporter to handle, responses will be capped, so it's best to respond early. If the reporter follows up with you, respond quickly. Reporters are more likely to build long-term relationships with sources they can count on to be timely and accurate.

If you would like to proactively position your company's leaders as experts in their fields, well-placed links on Twitter, Facebook, and Linkedin can help build respect and trust. However, if members of the media aren't among your friends, fans, or followers, you may not be reaching the right audience to garner publicity. Although social media is the newest way to connect, attracting members of the press to join the groups that receive your social media messages usually requires old-fashioned networking and relationship building.

If your company leaders can speak knowledgeably about a local current event, call a reporter, but first organize and rehearse some talking points so they can speak logically and concisely about the issue. You can also write letters to the editor or guest editorials in the local newspaper or secure speaking engagements at local community groups to establish expertise.

After a media outlet features your company, don't forget to extend the impact of the publicity by posting links to the story on your blog and website pressroom.

What Qualifies as News?

Different media outlets, including online outlets, view the newsworthiness of stories differently. Sometimes your company's news will stand alone. Other times, you may be part of a bigger story, such as a "trend" story on the housing market, home design, or community revitalization. Becoming part of larger news stories is never guaranteed, but several strategies already discussed in this chapter will help reporters find you and remember you: old-fashioned networking and relationship-building, registering as a source for HARO queries, and publishing press releases with keywords. Although the first two methods require proactively reaching out to reporters (only under the right conditions on HARO), the latter one helps reporters find you if they're searching for a particular topic online. You will want to make sure you have plenty of online releases incorporating lots of relevant keywords so reporters can find you when they need you.

What kind of news should you publish? Following are typical topics home builders address in their press releases:

- Community groundbreaking or opening
- New model home
- Innovative floor plan or exterior design
- Green building or other specialized construction method
- Charitable activity
- Personnel change (new hire or promotion in key positions)
- Award (to a person or for a product)
- Achievement of professional designation

Whenever you can demonstrate innovation or show that you are setting a trend, excelling, or bringing change in the community, you have a story!

Building Relationships with Reporters

Old-fashioned face-to-face networking or getting online introductions through sites like Linkedin will help you get to know reporters. Old-fashioned customer service will keep them coming back. As with any customer relationship, you'll want to show them that you understand their needs and concerns. This means being accurate and timely, and providing the best possible product, such as well-written and complete information and photos.

Once the relationship is established, reporters may follow your Twitter feed or fan your Facebook page. Attracting media coverage for your company requires the same tenacity as attracting home buyers does.

Cost and Management of Social Media

I f it's free, why should I pay? Because "there's no such thing as a free lunch" definitely applies to the Internet. Social media programs require a significant investment of time and, usually, money.

However, building your marketing budget around a sound social media program and strategy will cost a fraction of what you previously spent on advertising. Work with a social media agency or consultant to create your strategy, build your sites, and tie everything together. A knowledgeable agency or consultant can coach your team along the way—explaining each site and best practices for social media optimization. By working with someone who has built multiple sites and already has experienced the learning curve, you will save money and increase your program's effectiveness. Expect to spend $3,000 to $5,000 to set up your sites, including a self-hosted WordPress blog that you own, and $1,000 to $5,000 per month (or more depending on factors such as the scope of your program) to maintain the sites and implement programs.

Why Can't My Niece Build My Facebook Page?

You wouldn't hire a person with little or no experience to paint your house. Likewise, social media marketing and social networking demand professional expertise. Having your niece build one or two social networking sites without an overall marketing strategy or anyone in your company working with her to find the right friends, fans, and followers will not increase traffic or conversations to help you build your business. Launching a program with a poorly built blog or no blog at all will make social media optimization daunting. Make sure that the person or team you choose to build your SMM program thinks, plans, and mobilizes strategically. You will be even farther ahead of your competition if you work with a team with a social media track record.

Through the World Wide Web, you can either create fabulous curb appeal for your company or drive potential buyers away with a virtual front door that opens up to a confusing plan or no design at all. Remember, like any marketing effort, SMM should be strategic, have measurable goals, and complement your overall marketing and branding efforts.

Managing Social Media

Consider who will manage your social networking strategy. The marketing director? Sales manager? Online sales counselor? Receptionist? Sales team? An outside agency? You can enlist a combination of team members. Your company's size will determine the answer, but a blend of internal and external management works well for most companies. No matter who manages the hands-on tactics, you need one person to lead and direct the strategy and keep the marketing on track. Often, the sales team, online sales counselor, or marketing director can take the lead answering questions and engaging customers and potential buyers on social networking sites. Meanwhile, behind the scenes, a consultant or social media marketing company facilitates the team and either builds the sites or oversees site setup and trains the internal team to use sites.

Outsourcing

Look at many types of companies because every agency has unique capabilities. Do you need a firm to teach you how to converse with customers online in a meaningful way? Are you interested in driving traffic to your blog and website through SMO? Do you want to maintain a crisp brand image and promise online? Avoid making a costly mistake. Understand the necessary skills to build an effective social media program. Following are eight critical questions to consider in evaluating the competency of a social media marketing consultant, agency, or team.

1. **Do they have a blog?** If a company or consultant is to build an effective blog for your company, it must have experience building and running its own blogs successfully. Most seasoned social media marketers who can prove ROI understand how to build your program with the blog as the engine. An experienced consultant will have been blogging and building blogs since 2006 or 2007.

2. **When you Google the company or consultant's name, what do you find?** A seasoned social media marketer should have pages of search results mentioning the company name and their personal name. How can you trust your online reputation to a company if it has not created a positive reputation of its own?

3. **What social networking sites does the company or consultant use?** If they believe in social media, they should be active on sites including Twitter, Facebook, Linkedin, Trulia, ActiveRain, YouTube, Google+, and many others. They will have a port-

folio reflecting many years of contributing to these sites.

4. **What is the suggested strategy for using social media to achieve your overall marketing objectives?** A competent social media marketer can build a strategy that works for your team. Social media marketing is not one-size-fits-all. Your goals will probably vary greatly even from those of your closest competitors. Your strategy should be part of an overall marketing plan.

5. **What training will the company or consultant offer to you and your team?** They should be able to train your team to use various sites and tools with training materials they have developed. They should be able to answer your questions or know where to find the answers.

6. **Does the company or consultant understand SEO?** Social media success is measured by traffic to your blog and website, and your ability to capture leads. Without SEO, you won't maximize these three areas. What is the web presence of the company or consultant you are considering hiring? Glancing at the title tags on their website, blog, or both, will tell you.

7. **Can the company show you examples of its clients with netweaving?** The ability to interconnect all of your sites increases their effectiveness exponen-

tially. Ask for examples of clients with netweaved social media sites.

8. **What return will you get from your investment in hiring the company or consultant?** Will they provide reports, or at least advice on what to measure? How will they know what is working and what isn't?

Effective social media and search engine marketing starts with strategy and drives through implementation. You would not trust your brand identity and the *Four Ps* of marketing to someone new to your industry, so why would you trust your online brand image to someone without a proven online history and track record? Understanding product, price, place, and promotion, and a fifth P—people—is critical to success in social media marketing.

Time Commitment

Most companies should plan to devote about 20 hours a week to blogging, posting, and conversing with potential clients. Of course, your strategy could include more or less time. If you are a large company with a big marketing program, your social media program will take longer. Posting to your blog typically accounts for half the time needed.

"Team blogging works well when you have a strong lead blogger. The lead blogger writes most of the blog content and other team members contribute ideas and post occasionally. One person must be responsible for the blog," says David L. Owen, president, Boone Homes, Inc.

Choosing Sites and Developing Content

Your social media strategy could incorporate 3 sites or 30. After you have set goals and a budget for your program, you can determine how many sites to target. The basic sites for any successful campaign are a self-hosted WordPress blog, Facebook, YouTube, and Twitter. Following are three examples of what a program might encompass, based on company size and market(s):

Small-Volume Builder

Blog. Post stories on your blog twice a week. Make sure to invite other members of your team to contribute information such as the following:

- **Community information.** Focus on your specific neighborhood or the greater area. If your neighborhood is next to the most popular ice cream

store in the area, mention it. Don't forget community amenities and nearby shopping and restaurants. Isn't that new sushi restaurant down the
street great?

- **Home plans.** Mention interesting features such as
second-floor laundry rooms, two-and-a-half-car
garages, docking stations, large pantries, spa bathrooms, and flex space. Write your post so readers
can feel what it is like to live in one of your
homes ("You'll enjoy having a cup of coffee on
the back deck overlooking the adjacent golf
course.").

- **Home maintenance tips.** Provide advice on
cleaning the gutters, caulking a tub, having the
HVAC serviced, cleaning the clothes dryer vent,
and recognizing signs of insect infestation. You
could provide a maintenance list for each season,
or discuss how to tackle one chore on the list
step-by-step.

- **Mortgage information and trends or other housing information.** Buying a home can be confusing, even if you have previously purchased one.
Help your buyers to feel more comfortable with
the process by telling them what to expect. Review the steps for a loan application, tell buyers
how to get a copy of their credit score, and explain different types of loans.

● **Low-maintenance living.** Every builder has a slightly different interpretation of what low-maintenance living is. Therefore, define it—from exterior lawn care to painting and pressure washing the exterior, to snow removal.

Facebook. Update your Facebook status at least once or twice a week. Have your sales manager congratulate agents on recent sales and announce activities and events in your communities on Facebook. Include photos and albums of communities, homes, and events.

Twitter. Follow all the agents you can find in your area and interact with them. Tweet thanks to them for bringing in home buyers, retweet their interesting posts and comment on their posts. Then expand your interaction to local restaurants and boutiques. Nobody wants to talk to themselves on Twitter. After you form relationships, converse, and retweet their news, they will start retweeting yours as well.

YouTube. Recruit a real estate agent to help you shoot video of your homes, communities, and happy home owners. Try to post one video per month. You can also post videos on your blog or Facebook page. Those happy home owners who just bought their second home from you would make a great video testimonial. Consider having an agent give a tour of one of the homes you recently completed; they could even interview the builder about favorite features of the home.

Campaign. Give to a nonprofit. Offer $1 for every new Facebook Like for a limited time or until you get a predetermined number of new fans. You can request that the potential beneficiary of your campaign promote it as well. Use all of your social media sites to promote the campaign but make sure they link to your Facebook page or blog. Several builders have donated to charities during the holidays using this strategy. Make sure to connect with the nonprofit before you start this type of campaign. If you find a social-media-savvy nonprofit, they will often help you promote the campaign through their sites and newsletters.

S&A Homes added a Salvation Army campaign to its Facebook page during the holidays. The builder donated one dollar for every new Like on the page. The company also added a Salvation Army app that allowed Facebook visitors to donate directly to the Salvation Army from the S&A Homes page.

Production Builder

Blog. Publish two or more stories a week (some builders post five days a week) as follows:

- **Promote your city.** Perhaps it recently made a top 10 list or is recognized for its quality of life.
- **Focus a series of posts around themes.**
  - First time home-buying tips that answer questions about issues such as mortgages, contracts, and taxes
  - Home organization from kitchens to garages and how your homes help organize buyers' lives
  - Energy efficiency, including how your homes reduce energy bills, and tips for further savings.
- **Add videos** of all of your communities or individual home plans.
- **Discuss your credentials,** including ENERGY STAR certification, and awards your company, homes, communities, or staff have won.

Facebook. Most production builders have set up one corporate Facebook page and a series of city-specific pages for the markets where they build homes. Often these builders find the best results by having the corporate marketing department run the corporate page and selecting an online sales counselor or sales manager to run their city-specific Facebook page. Post about your events, sales, area attractions, and new restaurants and shops near your communities.

Twitter. Tweet about incentives, sales, events, and area attractions. Connect with agents, mortgage bankers, and local retailers, and promote their events. They will promote yours in return. For example, you might tweet that the local cupcake store is offering two-for-one cupcakes today and that while they are in the area cupcake lovers should stop by your sales center: 2-4-1 cupcakes at @GigisCupcakestoday, stop by Name of Community for water and a tour while u r there (link to community's website).

Chances are that the cupcake store will retweet your tweet.

For an incentive, try something like: Going, Going, Gone. Today only free frig w/purchase of Name of Home Model at Community (link to community's website).

YouTube. Video possibilities are limited only by your imagination. Include model home tours, community walks, amenities in use, home owner testimonials, and people enjoying your events. Interview co-op agents who have sold more than one of your homes in a year about why they like working with you and what buyers like about your homes.

Campaigns. How about offering a free refrigerator or a similar option or upgrade to any buyer who checks into your community on Foursquare or a similar site? You also can offer percentage-off or dollars-off coupons to buyers who Like, follow, or check in to your community.

Custom Builder

Blog. Position yourself as the expert on luxury living in your city. Post photos of your amazing homes with your blog posts. Create content that ensures customers will choose you to build their custom home. You can discuss owner's suites; wine cellars; pools and spas; outdoor kitchens; home theaters; man caves; garages; exteriors; and windows and doors.

Support a local charity and ask your readers to participate with you. Sterling Custom Homes asked people to Like its Facebook page. For every new Like, the builder donated one dollar to the Make-A-Wish Foundation® of Central and South Texas. The builder gained 100 new fans and gave to a local charity. The Make-A-Wish Foundation promoted the program in its local newsletter.

Showcase homes under construction with photos and video. Consider shooting a walk-through video of the home at framing, drywall, and when the finishes start going in. These photos can pique the interest of potential buyers for the home or your next project. Make sure the images do justice to all of the details you include in the trim, fixtures, and finishes.

Facebook. Add the mobile Facebook application to your smartphone so you can post updates no matter where you are. Having the mobile app makes it so easy to respond to questions on your Facebook page from anywhere, change your status to reflect news, or add photos. Use your smartphone to snap a photo of a newly completed kitchen and upload it to your Facebook page with a post saying, "We just finished the kitchen at 1111 Gorgeous Home Drive in Neighborhood. Please call to tour the home." Or even a closing update, "We just closed another home. Congratulations to the new home owners at 1111 Gorgeous Home Drive." Consider posting photos grouped by each area of the home to protect your home owner's privacy. Your high-end home owners don't want everyone that frequents your Facebook page to be able to tour their home room by room. Instead, create photo albums of many homes and group the photos by room or area, such as game rooms, pools, outdoor living, exterior elevations, gardens, living rooms, casitas, master suites, kitchens, and other areas. Reach out to real estate agents and your happy home owners and ask them to Like your page. Strive to update your Facebook page once a week with a new blog post, a comment about a home under construction, more photos, or information on your current campaign.

Twitter. Add a mobile Twitter application to your smartphone so you can tweet while you wait for lunch, or dinner, or in a grocery store line. Here are some examples:

- Home at 1111 Gorgeous Home Drive sold today, congratulations to the new owners. (link to photo of home)
- It was nice to see <u>Agent Name</u> at our home today. Thanks for touring it with your customers
- We just finished all the landscaping at 1111 Gorgeous Home Drive; now it's ready for move in (link to home on website)

Include photos and links in your tweets and update your followers on projects and available home features. Twitpic (http://twitpic.com/) allows Twitter users to upload photos and video. You simply attach the photo to the tweet and Twitpic will incorporate it with a link to the image or video.

YouTube. Video is a great way for an out-of-town home owner to follow the progress of a home under construction. Shoot footage and upload it to YouTube so your home owners can review it. You can restrict viewers so only people you invite can see it. You can also shoot footage of homes under construction that are for sale and place those on your public YouTube channel.

Remodeler

Blog. Update your blog at least weekly and monitor it for comments. Following are some blog content ideas:

- Before and after photos of completed projects
- Tips for consumers considering a remodeling project
- Great products you've used in your projects and how they function
- Problems you have solved for home owners with remodeling, such as making a bathroom accessible for aging in place
- Your designations, such as Certified Green Professional (CGP), Certified Aging in Place Specialist (CAPS), or Graduate Master Builder (GMB)

Facebook. Ask the people you want to follow you to connect. It's simple, but have you done it yet? To garner more referrals, incorporate a request for happy customers to Like you on Facebook into your closeout procedures for your remodeling projects.

If you've just started your Facebook page, send an e-blast to all of your clients asking them to follow your blog, Like you on Facebook, and follow you on Twitter. Exercise discretion with email to avoid being labeled a spammer or breaking the law. Use an email marketing program with an opt-out function like Mail-

Chimp (www.mailchimp.com), ConstantContact (www. constantcontact.com), or iContact (www.icontact.com) to help you comply with the CAN-SPAM Act. You should also

- Know the law
- Discuss the law with your attorney
- Monitor email sent on your behalf

You are liable for your email messages even if you have hired another company or person to send email on your behalf.

Follow local real estate agents on Facebook and Twitter and ask them to follow you too. Many of the homes they sell will need remodeling.

Add photo albums for every project with before and after pictures and maintain photo albums by project type as well, such as bathrooms, kitchens, and additions.

Twitter. Create a Twitter account to tweet from your blog posts and to engage with real estate agents. To generate interest in following you, tweet valuable content, including tips on planning for a successful remodeling project. Link each tweet to your website or blog. Tweet about your remodeling passions, whether they are redesigning a kitchen, incorporating green features, creating luxurious master suites, or enabling home owners to age in place.

YouTube. Videotape happy remodeling clients giving testimonials about your craftsmanship. You can load the videos on your blog and embed them in e-blasts.

Campaigns. Everyone wants a great deal. From Groupon to Facebook to Foursquare, consumers are looking for coupons. What do you offer them to connect with you? Add a coupon to your blog or Facebook page for

- a free initial consultation;
- a free sink with a kitchen remodel; or
- 10% off an outdoor kitchen when you schedule by a certain date.

Social couponing sites are hot. Consumers want a good deal and they are willing to work to get it. Sites like Groupon offer daily deals of 50% to 90% off on products and services.

Product Supplier

Blog. Publish new stories on your blog twice a week. Engage readers with lively prose, instead of just announcing a product release. For example, Construction Resources introduced its new frieze carpet as follows: "Frieze Carpeting: Shag Remixed? Can a remix ever be better than the original? It doesn't often happen that way in music, but when it comes to carpeting, frieze carpet has definite advantages over its older cousin, shag."

Here are some product topics worth blogging about:

- New product launches, new colors, new design elements or features
- Events, including open houses, online sales, and spring tent sales
- Eco-friendly, energy-saving, or other green product options
- Solutions for every price point
- On-time delivery and customer service, including testimonials
- Photos of completed installations

Facebook. Promote your events in advance and then follow up by posting photos. Remember to tag people who attend so the photo is on their page too. Post product news in an interesting way. For example, rather than writing a blatant sales pitch like "We have new frieze carpet in stock," use a rhetorical question and engage readers like this: "Remember shag carpet? Well, it's back in fashion, only now it's called frieze and it comes in much fresher colors. Please share your shag carpet memories with us."

Twitter. Follow your customers on Twitter and retweet their successes. Tweet about customer installations and cutting-edge aspects of your product, such as green features, aging-in-place functionality, low VOCs, recycled content, or time savings. Always link to your website, blog, or both, in your tweets.

YouTube. Showcase your product using video, from how it's made to how it's used to how it can solve specific problems. Include customer testimonials in your video library.

Campaigns. Why not offer a free sink if a customer buys 40 linear feet of countertop? Or a free spice pullout with a new set of kitchen cabinets? Perhaps you could offer an upgrade on a faucet or toilet. Can you add an extra year of warranty? A free evaluation? A free spring HVAC check-up or other service? You are probably already offering specials like this, so add the buzz to your social sites.

Developing Content

Rich, relevant content is critical to attracting fans, followers, and visitors. Content demands planning. Your editorial calendar should include upcoming press releases, email blasts, newsletter stories, blog posts, and the content you plan to post to Facebook, Twitter, Pinterest, Linkedin, and Google+. When you create these items, repurpose them on online public relations sites and other blogs. Set your blog to syndicate content to your Facebook page and your Twitter account. These step-savers will ensure your social networking efforts are efficient.

Include news, award announcements, educational features, and community interest information in your press releases and blogs. Consumers are interested in specials, new products and services, how-tos, local information, and other topics. Answer WIFM in your content, tailoring subject matter for the particular audiences you want to reach. Your content must meet their needs or they won't follow you or engage you in conversation.

Social Media Policy

Now that your company is embracing social media, you need to create a *social media policy*. Your policy should discuss why you are using social media and explain the goals of your social media strategy. A list of "don'ts" is not a comprehensive policy. Your policy should address employee behavior online, in general and specifically on social networking sites, especially as it relates to the company. Mashable recommends addressing the following 10 areas in a social media policy:[38]

- Explain the purpose of social media.
- Be responsible for what you write.
- Be authentic.

- Consider your audience.
- Exercise good judgment.
- Understand the concept of community.
- Respect copyright and fair use.
- Protect confidential proprietary information.
- Add value.
- Be productive.

Your company's social media policy should be unique, reflecting your culture and brand. Some companies are more liberal than others in who they allow to post and participate in their social media efforts. Neither a liberal nor a conservative approach is right or wrong.

As you make decisions like choosing the team to manage your social media marketing, remember the most important "rule" with SMM is consistency. Choose the team that can keep your program on track daily, weekly, and for the long haul.

Avoiding Pitfalls

Social media marketing has ramifications as well as rewards. The exponential nature of Internet communication can prove to be both a blessing and a curse. If you participate on third-party websites (sites you do not own), you are posting information that you cannot remove. Each blog post, tweet, and conversation will be seen by many users.

Self-Promotion

Shameless self-promotion never works well, but it is especially poorly received on social networking sites, where participants want to interact with their friends and favorite brands. Unlike *push advertising,* your posts should be conversational and provide interesting or valuable information to your community without overtly asking for a sale. Think of how you'd feel at a cocktail party if every time you turned around the same person handed you a business card and gave you a one-liner on his or her product or service. Social networking is no different! People are much more likely to friend, fan, or follow the person who provides useful information than the one who is always selling something.

One way to encourage interaction is to ask a question in your post. For example, rather than posting, "Facebook has changed the way it does feeds: There are now two options—top news and most recent," you might post "Facebook has changed its feeds to top news and most recent. I like the top news. Which do you like better?" Apply this same concept to posts about your communities, homes, remodeling projects, and news. For instance: "We've added new lower calorie menu items. Do you want to know the calorie count and more about these healthier options?"

Post with Discretion

Don't post or message too often. Often participants in social networks will accept your invitation to be your friend, fan, or follower for only a day or two. They try before they buy. But after a few days, they get tired of constantly finding your Facebook emails, incessant posts, and inappropriate tweets, so they walk away. Unfortunately, they are walking away from a relationship with your company.

On the other hand, some companies launch a disjointed social media presence without a strategy for maintaining their connections. Because social media then becomes too difficult or time-consuming to manage, they walk away from it. Abandoning your social media sites sends a negative message. Your contacts, friends, and followers may wonder if your business is struggling or defunct. Therefore, before you begin blogging, tweeting, and searching for networks, have a plan in place and a commitment to generating content that will build a positive brand.

Don't be afraid to cheer on your contacts. Like their posts on Facebook and retweet good tweets. Participate in the community by sharing but ensure you are up-to-date on the *netiquette* for each site so you don't respond inappropriately! For example, having an unfinished profile is a terrible offense on most sites. Don't start posting anywhere until you have built out your site. Posting without photos, descriptions, URLs, and contact information is like going to a networking event without business cards: you are unlikely to get follow-up.

Don't Be a Snark

The Urban Dictionary defines *snark* as a combination of "snide" and "remark," in other words, a sarcastic comment, or a person who makes one. Don't be a snark, even though becoming the target of a snark may be inevitable. (*Forbes* magazine says the unhappy consumer group of *badvocates* represents about 20% of the world's adult population online and each one communicates his or her bad feelings to 14 people.[39])

Visiting http://www.RippOffReport.com, http://www.Yelp.com, http://www.city-data.com/forum/, or any number of other websites reveals the power of unhappy consumers. Because they are already conversing online even if you aren't there to hear it, you need to create places to embrace happy customers. Engage with both groups. Communication is the most important step toward building brand, creating transparency, and improving customer service.

7

Promoting Your Brand Online

Once you have built a team, written a plan, created a blog, improved your search results, and begun to use social networking sites, you are ready to netweave your online presence and promote it. Identify your objectives, the audiences you wish to reach, and where those people go online. Each company will adopt a unique strategy based on location, product or service, pricing, and other factors.

Companies often use free social networking sites to spread the word about other facets of their social media programs. Just keep in mind that your goal is to use social media to build your business, not just to network because it's fun. Although social networking *is* fun, without goals it can also waste time and squander resources.

Every time you touch people online you make a brand impression. Impressions are also created when consumers visit your social sites. Whether it is a good impression or a bad impression depends on the quality of the interaction and how well you fulfill your company's brand promise. Take these seven steps to leave a good impression:

1. **Brand all of your sites with your colors, logo, and information.** Make sure visitors know they are visiting your official sites. For example, the Traton Homes logo is clearly displayed in the upper left hand corner of the Marietta, Georgia-based company's website and blog. Wherever it appears, the company logo uses consistent colors of red, blue, and tan.

2. **Develop messaging.** What is your brand promise? Whatever it is, make sure that everyone in the company understands the message and can successfully convey it to others on the spot face-to-face, on the phone, and in email. Traton Homes stresses value by promising "Altogether More" (quality, location, lifestyle, and value) and longevity ("since 1971") in its brand promise.

   Kimberly Garwood, marketing manager of Traton Homes, says the "Altogether More" message affects everyone's job, from land development through design and construction, to sales and marketing. "Value is at the center of all of our process, messaging, and communication efforts," Garwood says.

3. **Post regularly on your social sites.** There is noth-

ing worse than visiting a social site that has lain dormant for months. Don't starve your social media program through neglect. This implies that you may be out of business. "A corporation just launching a social media site should be aware that there is more to the process than just launching a site. It is an ongoing commitment that requires expertise and consistent development as it becomes a staple part of your marketing efforts," Garwood says. Chris Schoonmaker, vice president of sales for S&A adds, "Make it easy, but be committed to keeping it up to date. You have to post regularly to keep it fresh. The sites can't sit stagnant for months. Making sure to keep it fresh keeps the momentum going."

4. **Post unique content that will help define your brand.** Whether you build green, 50+, entry-level, luxury, or remodel within a particular niche, your USP and your brand should be evident in your posts. "When you write more than 100 blogs about your company, you learn who you are, what your core competency is and what you do well. This gave us an excellent point to start from when we sat down to do the branding exercise. It made it easy because we absolutely know who we are," says Ashleigh Shetler, manager of sales and marketing development for S&A Homes in State College, Pennsylvania.

5. **Practice good customer service.** Make sure you respond to comments and questions on your social pages promptly, especially if they are negative, which they usually will not be. If you get a negative post, simply respond, "I'm so sorry you are having a problem, This is Name with Name of Company. Please call me at Direct-Dial Phone Number so I can help you." This type of response will defuse the problem, keep it from escalating on your social site, and move it back to your traditional channels for handling customer complaints.

6. **Understand that your customers control your brand.** Your company will impress them either positively or negatively each time they interact with it. This extends far beyond your advertising, logo, and Internet marketing to include phone calls, email, and the first introduction. Your customers need to know that they can trust your brand. "Social media has really forced builders to re-evaluate their entire marketing message—online, advertising, point of sale, product, everything. Because social media is so interactive, timely and up-to-date, it really forced S&A Homes to look at all of our advertising and take it to a more interactive level as well," Shetler says.

7. **Use a spokesperson, character, or icon to help define your brand.** It could be a supermodel or su-

perhero, but it could also be a lovable pooch. For example, Homer "works" for The Home Depot, Skates for the Chicago Wolves, and the Chick-fil-A cows for Chick-fil-A. You must admit that selling chicken sandwiches while focusing on cows is brilliant branding. Fully develop a persona and a voice for the spokesperson, whether a cartoon character or a live human being. Here are some examples of how to use a spokesperson as your number one brand advocate in social marketing:

Blogging. Give your spokesperson his or her own blog or a special category on your existing blog. They can discuss excellent customer service, special home features, community amenities, and home personalization.

Facebook. Update your corporate page to include your spokesperson in your company photo, perhaps standing in front of one of your homes or sitting inside the home he or she bought from you. If your spokesperson appears around town, mention the location in your status updates.

YouTube. Shoot videos or incorporate your spokesperson into videos with your sales agents, superintendents, and other staff. As your brand advocate, a spokesperson can interview happy home owners, and interject positive comments as an owner of one of your homes.

Twitter. Have your brand spokesperson take over your Twitter account once a week, and share messages or host a Twitter chat.

"We probably approached this differently than many builders because instead of starting with a branding campaign, we started by building our social media program. We then realized how well it worked and that we needed to do this well with everything else we do. Now we have integrated social media through all of our advertising messages, including point of sale," Shetler says.

She says it worked out well to start rebuilding marketing with a quality social media program. "We may not have as many followers, but the ones we have are really loyal. We have slowly and steadily built up our numbers of followers on the blog and Facebook," Shetler says. "Now we are working to establish a two-way street between the blog and the website, so that both are strong online presences. It goes to show that it doesn't really matter where you are in the process, you can make social media work for you. When we first got started, we were really concerned that our website was not where it needed to be, but mRELEVANCE helped us build a strong social media program, and the state of the website didn't matter."

What are Shetler's tips for home builders getting ready to launch a social marketing program? "Make sure that whoever is responsible for implementing your social media program has a good handle on the company from finance to sales, marketing, events, who the company is, and what is going on in the company," she advises.

It can take years to build a brand and fulfill a brand promise. Whenever a consumer shops for or purchases a product or service from your company, they encounter your brand and it makes an impression. Therefore, it is worth taking the time to build your brand right. Social marketing makes it easier than ever to either build or destroy your brand.

Maximizing Email and Newsletters

Use the following strategy to manage your email and newsletter content and house it on the web:

- Post all of your content on your blog.
- Choose a few provocative sentences, or *teasers,* from each article to populate your newsletter template. Link to the complete story in the blog from these teasers.

- Use an email service that allows you to send HTML newsletters or one like Mail Chimp that will easily convert your blog's RSS into a newsletter.

- Make sure the program you use will track clicks and opens. Tracking will show you who is most interested in your new product, service, new incentive, or other company news.

- Include links to all of your social media sites in your newsletter so readers can connect, follow, and like you on their chosen sites. Also, incorporate *social sharing* in your email marketing so recipients can forward email content to their social networks. This will expand your newsletter's reach. Place social sharing links to popular social networks such as Twitter, Digg, Reddit, StumbleUpon, Facebook, Linkedin, and Yahoo! Buzz in your email. A study by the email marketing company GetReponse found that email messages with social sharing options get a 30% higher click-through rate than emails without options for sharing.[40] According to Marketing Sherpa, 80% of marketers agree that social sharing extends email content to new potential customers and increases brand awareness.[41]

The Home Builders Association of Greater Springfield (fig. 7.1) creates its weekly newsletter using stories from its blog (http://www.springfieldhba.com/) and pulling the content in via RSS feed to MailChimp. Traffic to its website spikes for several days after the company distributes the newsletter.

Social Media on Your Website

Include social media icons with links on your website as well to make it easy for potential buyers to find information about your company. Consider displaying your company's telephone number on your home page. This communicates that you are out in front and ready to interact.

Also place links to social media sites in your email signatures. You don't have to include all of them you participate in, just enough to point readers in the right direction. The four basic sites to include are typically your blog, Facebook, Twitter, and YouTube.

Your blog also should prominently display links to your social media sites as on Atlanta, Georgia-based Edward Andrews Homes blog (fig. 7.2), http://eahhomesblog.com. Because this blog is separate from the main website, the builder made sure that it provides a clear link to the main website. Link all or most blog posts to a page on your website.

Figure 7.1 Home Builders Association of Greater Springfield newsletter

Using blog stories as the basis for your newsletter saves time and streamlines the process while maximizing your ROI. (Source: Reprinted with permission from The Home Builders Association of Greater Springfield, Springfield, Missouri)

Figure 7.2 **Edward Andrews Homes**

Visitors to the Edward Andrews Homes blog easily find links to all of the home builder social media sites. (Source: Reprinted with permission from Edward Andrews Homes, Atlanta, Georgia)

Make it easy for people to engage with your social networks. For example, the Construction Resources website features Facebook prominently on the home page; visitors can Like the Facebook page without leaving the site (fig. 7.3).

Even with the mass migration online, you still use print for some things. Include your social networking sites on yard signs, billboards, and business cards. When you comment on other companies' blogs and sites, include your website's URL to ensure that your post links back to your site.

Figure 7.3 **Facebook like button**

One way to increase your company's following on Facebook is to add a Facebook Like box to your corporate website. (Source: Reprinted with permission from Construction Resources, Inc., Atlanta, Georgia)

Social Media and Customer Relationship Management (CRM)

When potential buyers become friends, fans, or followers on social networking sites, they typically will observe more often than they participate. By giving you access to a Twitter, Facebook, or other online profile, they're saying they're willing to listen and may want to talk, but they are not permitting you to add them to your database to send junk mail or spam.

Social media is typically thought of as marketing, but I want to challenge you to think about social media as a way to build a bigger sales funnel for your business. Interacting with customers and clients in order to convert them from leads to prospects and then from prospects into buyers is the main goal of marketing and sales.

The typical interactive marketing program is built around your main messages, USPs, and assets—your website and blog. Social media sites including your blog,

Facebook, Twitter, Google+, Pinterest, Linkedin, and YouTube accounts can help to spread your marketing messages. When you also have an effective CRM program to capture qualified leads that come to your website, you can effectively focus your sales activities according to each individual buyer. Using an effective CRM program in combination with social media will provide you with a competitive advantage. Think about having a bigger sales funnel. It's not just new customers I'm talking about: social CRM can help you retain existing customers, too. Remember that consumers participate in group think and consult with trusted advisers (friends) on purchases they plan to make. By discovering and leveraging relationships among your buyers, your social CRM program will provide a more effective way to move leads and prospects through the sales funnel to become customers.

Buying Signals

In typical CRM systems, potential home buyers are categorized as leads, prospects, or customers. Your CRM system should recognize these different types of consumers by maintaining various types of lists. For example, interacting with a potential customer on Facebook does not give you the right to put them in your CRM program and send them marketing e-blasts. You could, however, add them to your CRM system with a note that they like your corporate Facebook page. You could then keep track of your interactions with them there. Be careful not to turn off friends, fans, followers, or people who Like you by sending them marketing information before they opt to receive it.

Be attentive, however, to subtle buying signals that may emerge in your interactions on Facebook. For example, someone might request information about today's special or your operating hours. These simple requests indicate the fan, friend, or follower is starting to think about purchasing from you. This signals that you can add the person to your CRM system. Send a personal email message sharing the benefits of receiving further correspondence from you and ask permission to send email messages. If they decline, put them in a category of your CRM system for potential buyers who should be contacted only through the social networking medium in which they initiated the contact.

One the biggest benefits of a CRM system is the ability to provide everyone in your organization with a 360-degree view of a prospect. Everyone knows where prospects have visited (in person and online) and is privy to the information collected about them. Consider budget, company size, and functional requirements in choosing among the many CRM programs available. Among programs to evaluate are: Builder 1440,

BuildTopia, Lasso, Microsoft Dynamics, Pivotal, SalesForce, Oracle, and Sales Simplicity.

Getting Social with CRM

The world is more social than ever. Social networks continue to transform how we do business and interact with customers from one-way conversations to an interactive web of conversations. Finding out customer interests and ways to relate to them on a personal level is more important than ever.

To provide more detailed information on prospects and streamline communications, CRM systems are adding social media solutions to their programs. Look for new applications that allow users to integrate Facebook, Linkedin, Twitter, and other sites into CRM. For example, at least one CRM system enables users to post updates to their social accounts directly from the application. It allows users to find connections between prospects, customers, and decision-makers; find new opportunities through introductions; invite contacts and prospects to join social media sites; and track customer sentiment and engagement in the prospect database. The sales staff can see where the most recent contact with a prospect occurred, whether on Facebook, by email, or through some other means, and what the prospect thinks of the company.

Follow-Up and Customer Service

Who will manage the company's responses to social media comments and questions depends entirely on the organization. Knowledge of social media is not the only prerequisite. People who interact with consumers online should have the following attributes:

- **Aptitude for customer service.** Your customer service representative, online sales counselor, or a technology-savvy agent already trained to work with the public would be good choices. The person must have a can-do attitude toward customers.

- **Skill and comfort with new technology.** Interacting through social websites requires not only familiarity with the sites as they exist now, but interest in emerging applications and in devices such as smartphones and digital cameras.

- **Rapid response time.** People converse at the speed of life on social sites, and life moves quickly in today's technology-saturated world. In this context, a timely response means minutes, rather than hours. Failing to respond quickly could be the difference between a happy customer and a lost sale.

- **Solid grasp of the company's brand and USP.** To interact with customers, you want to make sure the person posting and answering their questions knows the answers to the questions that are most likely to be asked and can answer them in a way that keeps the customer personally engaged. There is nothing that consumers like less than being "sold" over a social network.

How to Measure Results

You can easily measure ROI if you know where to look for the information and which metrics are important to you. Much of it will be in website tracking reports created at regular intervals by most Internet marketing firms. Google Analytics allows websites to track visitors from the social sites and see their traffic patterns within a website. This data helps you identify which social sites are sending the best quality traffic to your main website.

Review your analytics and trend reports monthly and yearly. An effective program will show slow, steady growth with some seasonal variation and sensitivity to economic conditions.

Ideally the messages your company distributes through social media outlets are reaching target audiences and will produce measurable results. How you measure your social media campaign's success depends on your goals. Following are suggestions for measuring ROI compared with the five goals for a social media marketing strategy discussed in chapter 2: increasing website traffic, social media optimization, reputation management, engagement, and building brand.

Goal 1: Increasing Website Traffic

After you implement the strategies discussed in this book, has the number of unique visitors to your site increased? Look behind and beyond the numbers. A plan to post significant content online with links referring to the company's main website probably was part of the strategy for reaching this goal. If the plan has been successful, your site visitors will come from a wider variety of searches and a larger number of referring URLs. You also may see more first-time site visitors than returning visitors.

Often, visitors who find your site through items you've posted or conversations you've started will be comparatively higher quality traffic: they visit more individual pages and spend more time on your site than other visitors. My own experience has shown that visitors who link to the mRELEVANCE LLC (http://www.mrelevance.com) site from our tweets tend to spend more time exploring the site than visitors from Facebook. Visitors from social media sites tend to spend three to six minutes on a site. Visitors from Twitter spend more time because they are coming with less information: they have based their visit on a 140-character tweet instead of a longer post on Facebook or on your blog.

Measurements for Goal 1: Increasing Website Traffic

1. Number of unique visitors
2. Time visitors spend on site
3. Number of pages visitors view
4. Number of referring URLs
5. Number of visitors who click through to "Contact Us" section
6. Increase in traffic from the search engines

Goal 2: Social Media Optimization

An SMO strategy focuses on increasing the number of relevant keywords that direct the search engines to your site and the number of referring sites that direct traffic to your site. Expand your keyword searches as follows:

- Identify the terms site visitors already use to find the company.
- Develop a list of USPs that visitors might use to find you through a search engine.

Post content focusing on these words in various places, and link to your site with anchor text. Include these keywords in your blog and other online posts.

You should see an increase in the number of keywords your website is relevant for, as well as the number of referring sites linking to your website. If the link is relevant and on highly visible sites, users are more likely to click it.

Measurements for Goal 2: Social Media Optimization

1. Number of keywords visitors use to find the site through search engines (fig. 9.1)
2. Quality of keywords (do they reflect the company's USP and are they commonly searched)
3. Number of referring sites (fig. 9.2)

Goal 3: Reputation Management

Businesses often undertake a reputation management program to push negative results from SERPs below the first screen or even deeper into search results. Posting positive, relevant content on online sites that rank

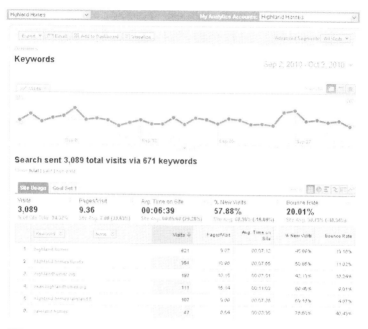

Figure 9.1 **Google Analytics results for Highland Homes**

Google Analytics shows that 671 different keywords found Highland Homes during a 30-day period. (Source: Reprinted with permission from Highland Homes, Lakeland, Florida)

highly in the search engines is an effective way to mitigate the negative publicity. How long it takes to improve first-page results depends on the power of the negative results.

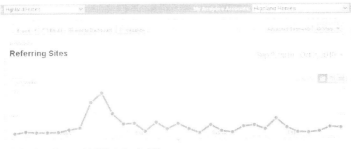

Figure 9.2 **Highland Homes referring sites**

Google Analytics shows that during a 30-day period, referring sites sent 1,986 visits from 224 sources to the Highland Homes website. (Source: Reprinted with permission from Highland Homes, Lakeland, Florida)

Measurements for Goal 3: Reputation Management

1. Proportion of company-generated information in page one search results

2. Negative search engine results moved to page two or lower of SERP

Goal 4: Social Networking

The goal of social networking is to engage target audiences in conversation. Specific target audiences will vary by company and may even vary by the social networking tool used. Most of these tools keep tabs on the people subscribing to the user's content, whether they call them friends, followers, or fans. The quality of your followers is much more important than the quantity. Therefore, if you aren't following people who can buy from you or influence the buying decision of a potential customer, rethink your strategy.

To monitor the conversation, you can create free alerts through Google Alerts to see what others are saying, or you can use a social media monitoring company. Many companies provide monitoring and the ability to post to social sites from a consolidated dashboard. Their services and prices vary, so research whether what they do will help you reach your goals. Some monitoring companies charge a flat monthly fee; others price their services by how many individuals you want to have logged in simultaneously and number of search queries.

You may want to consider the following social media monitoring companies:

- Alterian SM2
- BuzzStream
- HootSuite
- Meltwater News
- Radian 6
- Sprout Social
- Sysmos' Heartbeat
- Thrive
- Trakur
- Vocus

Measurements for Goal 4: Social Networking

1. Number of friends / followers / fans
2. Number of friends / followers / fans in your target audiences (for example home owners, real estate agents, home buyers, influencers)
3. Quality of conversations (Are friends / followers / fans just receiving content, or are they actually engaged and participating?)

Goal 5: Building Brand

Strategies for building brand are similar to those for SMO. You want to ensure that potential customers can find you online and that what they find represents your company honestly. If your company name is not unique, you must ensure that your brand appears high in the SERPs with a message that differentiates you from other companies with the same name.

Measurements for Goal 5: Building Brand

1. Combined measures for SMO and reputation management.
2. Increased USPs represented in keywords. If you are a green builder in Denver, for example, when local consumers search for green homes in Denver your company should rank high on the SERP.
3. Positive representations of the company in many places online.

Goal 6: Sales

If your social media program is successful in meeting goals 1–5, then you probably will achieve your ultimate goal: sales. With most home buyers researching markets and builders online, the entire social media network is influencing home sales. Following are three examples—a builder and two developers—that have translated social media into increased website traffic, more leads, and ultimately, more sales.

Highland Homes

Highland Homes of Lakeland, Florida, transformed a primarily print-based advertising campaign into an Internet-focused marketing campaign in 2008. Like all home builders faced with fewer sales, slower traffic, and reduced margins during the historic housing downturn, Highland Homes had to find ways to achieve sales with a smaller budget. By 2010, Highland Homes had cut its marketing budget by 80% but the company was still selling homes and even expanding, thanks to a strategic Internet-focused marketing program. In fact, the builder sold out a new community in 2012, averaging 45 contracts a month overall that year. The builder continues to cut its print spending and instead focuses on the company's blog, advertorials, email marketing, online display and PPC advertising, and news stories. In fact, the company didn't include any print advertising in its 2013 budget even though it will be entering three new submarkets, or smaller markets outside of the main market.

One interesting outcome is that Internet conversion has increased over the life of the program from 13% to more than 50%.

Highland Homes first hired mRELEVANCE in January 2008 to keep its website alive. The mRELEVANCE team rewrote the entire site in a different programming language, optimized the site for the search engines, and was in the midst of changing and updating the content when the home builder made a first round of budget cuts.

Kathie McDaniel of Highland Homes says, "The business intelligence provided by the monthly analytics reports from mRELEVANCE helps our team strategize on where to focus marketing dollars and time. As we focus on areas that are most effective, we have been able to increase our traffic to both our website and models while . . . increasing the Highland Homes brand. When our budget decreased, our biggest cutbacks were in print advertising—going from full-page, four-color weekly placements to quarter or half page, and now no print advertising."

At the same time, Highland Homes maintained a strong online presence with listing ads and banners in many places. One of the builder's top sources of traffic to its website is Google and Bing PPC advertising.

Strategy

To maintain brand, build online reputation, and enhance Highland Homes' search engine marketing, mRELEVANCE launched an SMM campaign. The campaign sought to use SMO to increase keywords and referring URLs for the Highland Homes website by

- building a blog;
- using external blogs;
- creating a Facebook page; and
- using other social networking, online public relations, and social bookmarking sites.

The blog launched as the news section of the builder's main website. It contains community news, events, and information on sales and the builder's team. Social networking sites, such as Facebook, Twitter, and ActiveRain, increased exposure within those communities. Online public relations sites filled the SERP results with positive news. Social bookmarking and email marketing supported the campaign.

Here are the year-over-year increases:

- Tremendous keyword growth from 188 in 2008 to 2,172 in 2012
- Steady increase in referring URLs from 74 in 2008 to 113 in 2012
- Explosive web traffic growth of unique visitors from 3,997 in 2008 to 15,419 in 2012

- More than 50% conversion rate of Internet leads to home purchase contracts in 2012 compared with 13% in 2009

Highland Homes has embraced social media as critical to its marketing strategy. "Since our marketing budget was cut we have definitely had to work smarter. Our social media campaign has given us a way to increase our SEO and traffic to our website, and interact with our buyers. mRELEVANCE keeps the strategy moving forward with blogs and posts, while the Highland Homes team tweets and posts the day-to-day news and sales stats," McDaniel says. "Our sales people have really embraced social media, and they are starting to convert Facebook interactions to sales." The company revamped its website to improve navigation and include more than one *call to action,* which increased the number of e-leads. "We have so many e-leads now that we are adding an online sales department to interact directly with these customers," McDaniel says.

The Highland Homes mobile site is a compact and comprehensive version of the Lakeland-based builder's main website. It provides general information about Highland Homes' communities, floor plan descriptions, pricing, contact information, and virtual tours. It is integrated with the builder's social media sites including Twitter, YouTube, and Facebook.

Benefits of the mobile site for consumers include

- fast load time on mobile devices;
- easy-to-view content with large fonts and graphics built for mobile; and
- minimal clicks required to view content—it's "finger friendly."

"With 10% to 15% of monthly site visitors on the Highland Homes website coming from mobile devices, it [was] the perfect time to create a site to accommodate those consumers," according mRELEVANCE managing partner, Mitch Levinson. "In just a couple short months, the new Highland Homes mobile site [had] already shown an increase in total website traffic to the builder's website by almost 15%. Based on the time viewing pages on the mobile site, these [were] new high quality buyers." Use the following three tips to optimize your marketing materials for mobile use:

1. **Keep it simple.** Since phone screens are small, Internet connections are slower, and users don't want to waste a lot of time, keep mobile websites and applications simple. Make them do fewer things, but better, than your regular site could.
2. **Be purpose driven.** Before creating your mobile site, ensure that it makes sense for your consumers.

Why, when, and where does your consumer use a device?

3. **Embrace mobile technology.** Instead of having consumers call a phone number or visit a site, use a QR code to allow them to quickly learn more about a service or product.

Follow these tips, and remember speed and usability are very important when designing a mobile site. Consumers using mobile devices are usually searching for something specific instead of just surfing the web.

B.F. Saul

B.F. Saul, the developer of Circle 75 Townhomes in Smyrna, Georgia, turned to SEO, social media, discounting, and a targeted Realtor e-flyer campaign in mid-2009 to propel the sale of its final 48 units.

The Circle 75 news blog (fig. 9.3) launched in July 2009 as the foundation of the social media and online marketing program. Using targeted keywords and SEO, the blog attracted more than 2,600 unique visitors and created a bigger lead funnel for converting Internet browsers to home buyers.

Traffic to the main Circle 75 website increased by more than 600% from January 2009 to January 2010 and more than 500% from February 2009 to February 2010.

Figure 9.3 Circle 75 blog

The Circle 75 Blog attracted a wide range of searches on a variety of keywords.
(Source: Reprinted with permission from B.F. Saul Company, Bethesda, Maryland)

Overall, website traffic during the campaign—from June 2009 to February 2010—increased by more than 400%.

The target market was first-time townhome buyers in Cobb County. Marketing objectives were straightforward: increase keywords, boost website traffic, and get more sales. The community sold out within eight months of launching the blog.

The blog improved the community's SEO by capturing more keywords for the main website (a 175% increase). Overall website traffic increased by more than 450%. The blog enhanced the community's Internet presence. Blog posts talked up the community and area events, highlighting attractions such as Smyrna Market Village and the community's hip Smyrna–Vinings location.

S&A Homes

S&A Homes actively builds homes in 65 communities throughout Pennsylvania and West Virginia. With a number of different product types and styles suitable for many demographics, S&A had to find a way to stretch its marketing dollars. The company hired mRELEVANCE to launch a social media marketing program. The campaign used online resources to showcase S&A homes, communities, and locations to increase the probability that today's technology-savvy home buyers and real estate agents would find S&A homes online, get to know the builder, and ultimately, buy an S&A home.

S&A Homes launched its social media campaign in July 2010 with three main goals:

1. Increase website traffic.
2. Create a place for consumers to converse with the builder.
3. Improve the SEO for its main website.

"We saw excellent early results. Within 45 days of launch the blog was already a top five referral source to our main website, with 75% of the traffic on the blog representing first-time visitors." said Ashleigh Shetler, manager of sales and marketing development for S&A Homes. "The blog continues to perform well. The blog was the number two referral site to our website with first-time visitors from the blog to the website representing 50% of the traffic [in 30 days]."

Google and Facebook are the top referring sites to the blog. Several other blogs and social media sites also send traffic to the blog, including Twitter. Keywords on the blog have grown from several dozen a month to more than 350 a month. Best of all, the blog metrics of visitors, keywords, referring sites, and overall traffic continue to grow each month.

S&A Homes Tool Kit

S&A Homes focused on four main social media tools:

1. **Blog** (http://www.sahomesblog.com/). The S&A Homes blog is built on a self-hosted WordPress platform. The blog's editorial calendar is planned several months out, and content focuses on topics from energy-efficient homes to tips for first-time buyers, home organization ideas, community events, and community news. The blogging team consists of members from both the S&A Homes team and mRELEVANCE. The blog's goal is to provide enticing content that also maximizes SEO. Blog categories include news, events, incentives, videos, testimonials, and locations. Each of these also has categories for S&A Homes' various community locations. The blog's home page features a video that allows visitors instant access to views of S&A homes.

2. **Facebook** (http://www.facebook.com/sahomes). We all want to go where everybody knows our name, and Facebook is definitely the neighborhood watering hole where everyone shares news and information. S&A Homes uses its Facebook page to connect with and engage home owners, home buyers, and real estate agents. Facebook content must be fresh, so S&A updates the page automatically

with blog news as well as posts unique to the Facebook page. The S&A Homes Facebook page invites first-time home buyers with a link to a comprehensive section on the company's blog that answers many questions that first-time buyers have. Hundreds of people Like the page and many of them actively participate by commenting, which makes the page feel like a community, rather than just a commercial website.

3. **YouTube** (http://www.youtube.com/SAhomebuilder). If a picture is worth a thousand words, a video must be worth a million. The S&A Homes YouTube page showcases communities and home plans. Many of these videos are embedded in blog posts as well. Sales agents can follow up with prospects by emailing them links to the videos.

4. **Twitter** (http://twitter.com/SAhomebuilder). S&A uses Twitter to further syndicate blog posts and promote campaigns, although the main focus of Twitter is to interact with agents and industry influencers. Future Twitter plans include promoting a lab home and e-home, as well as sharing first-time buying information.

Campaigns

Understanding that great content is not always enough to encourage online interaction, much less an action,

S&A Homes initiated several targeted social media campaigns to encourage online participation. The company has chosen to build a smaller, core group of followers who are genuinely interested in S&A Homes, instead of a larger group of followers who are just chasing companies for contest monies. Its campaigns reflect that philosophy:

- **$1,500 off Options and Upgrades.** The first campaign, a 45-day, $1,500-off options and upgrades promotion encouraged potential buyers to Like the S&A Homes Facebook page and download a coupon for $1,500 off S&A Homes options with the purchase of a new home (fig. 9.4). Buyers could use the coupon in conjunction with other incentives. Blog and Facebook posts, as well as email messages, promoted the campaign. When the promotion was over, customers had redeemed six coupons. You can read the blog post for the promotion at http://www.sahomesblog.com/2010/07/sa-homes-to-deliver-savings-to-facebook-fans/.

- **Operation Organize Simplify.** Building on the success of the coupon campaign, S&A Homes launched "Operation Organize Simplify" in mid October 2010. This campaign targeted potential home buyers and Realtors® with a multifaceted

Figure 9.4 **S&A Homes $1,500 upgrade incentive**

S&A Homes promoted its Facebook coupon through a blog post. (Source: Reprinted with permission from S&A Homes, State College, Pennsylvania)

program including blog posts (fig. 9.5), Facebook updates, and email blasts. "Operation Organize Simplify" focused on the benefits of home design to simplify one's life. Blog posts discussed kitchen storage, laundry rooms, charging stations, drop zones, and even the ultimate man cave—the garage.

To engage real estate agents and tap into their expertise, the blog asked them, "If you could build your dream home, what is the one organizational item that you would incorporate into every home?" Agents competed for a $150 gift card to a home improvement store and the opportunity to receive a $500 bonus at their next S&A Homes closing. Agents submitted creative organization strategies for Christmas tree rooms, kitchen electronics, and the ultimate mudroom.

Meanwhile, home buyers could download a coupon to redeem for $1,500 off organizational options on their presale new home purchase. Buyers redeemed six coupons during the 45-day campaign.

"After these home buyers signed contracts for their new homes, they took time to Like us on Facebook," Shetler said. This is big in terms of future referrals from these buyers via Facebook.

Figure 9.5 **S&A Homes Operation Organize Simplify**

S&A Homes promoted its Operation Organize Simplify campaign through the blog. (Source: Reprinted with permission from S&A Homes, State College, Pennsylvania)

You can view the Operation Organize Simplify blog post at http://www.sahomesblog.com/2010/10/how-do-you-organize-your-life/.

- **Life is Full of Firsts.** To demonstrate that buying a first home should be as special as a first kiss, first date, or your child's first day of school, S&A Homes launched "Life is Full of Firsts," geared toward educating first time buyers (fig. 9.6). Blog content aimed to demystify home buying for the first-timer by providing a "buying 101" primer that addresses topics such as FHA loans, mortgage interest deductions, USDA financing, the benefits of new construction instead of a used home, tax benefits of owning, and how to own with no money down. The Life is Full of Firsts promotion for first-time buyers is also set up as the Facebook landing page to encourage potential buyers to get the information they need and make educated home purchasing decisions.

Eight months after starting the social media program, S&A Homes reported the program performed better than the home builder expected. "Our social media program has exceeded our expectations. It has brought new visitors to our website, improved the SEO for our main website, created a place where consumers can have conversations and best of all, brought us buyers!"

says Shetler. "We had 12 home buyers redeem coupons for options and upgrades that they could have gotten only on our social media sites. There is no doubt that today's buyers are looking further than just our website. We will continue to provide them with ways to interact with us and reward them for their loyalty."

Meanwhile, central Pennsylvania home builder Keystone Custom Homes celebrated 20 years in business with a 20 Ways to Save campaign, a creative promotion that encouraged people to visit the builder's social sites for deals on new homes during a nearly seven-week period.

The builder offered coupons on its website, blog, Facebook, Twitter, and Pinterest pages. Incentives included a free stainless steel refrigerator, kitchen package upgrade, utility package upgrade, $1,000 off select floor plans or homes in select communities, free Whirlpool tub, deck upgrade, and other specials. Offers were available during limited time periods during the promotion period and could only be found on certain sites, which encouraged buyers to visit each site to find the one they most wanted to incorporate into their new dream home.

The campaign helped the builder connect with new home shoppers and get them to like, follow, and visit the sites and to stay connected online. The 53-day promotion raised the traffic originating from Facebook by more than 50%. On average, each visitor saw about 3.6 pages

Figure 9.6 S&A Homes Life is Full of Firsts campaign

S&A Homes educated first-time buyers through a campaign designed specifically for them. (Source: Reprinted with permission from S&A Homes, State College, Pennsylvania)

per visit and stayed for 5 to 10 seconds. Traffic from Twitter increased by 50% and traffic from Pinterest increased by almost 7%.

The promotion built momentum for Keystone, which was already experiencing a record sales year despite an economic recession. Customers redeemed 26 coupons, raising the builder's gross sales by 26% over the same period in 2011, from 53 to 67 homes. The most popular coupon (30% of the coupon redemptions), was posted only on the company's blog and was for a free 9 ft. basement upgrade. But customers redeemed coupons from all the sites, indicating that the campaign got shoppers visiting all of the builder's social media.

Crowdsourcing Special Events

It started with a few comments about kitchen appliances during #KBTribeChat, an online Twitter chat held on Wednesdays from 2 to 3 p.m. EST for kitchen and bath industry professionals. One interior design blogger challenged another to a cook-off. A grand idea was born for the 2012 Dwell on Design show in Los Angeles.

O'Reilly-DePalma and Flying Camel, two marketing communications agencies that were on the chat, jumped into action, organizing a live cook-off among bloggers in the Capital Ranges (a manufacturer of commercial-style kitchen ranges) booth. The set up included the two bloggers who started the challenge, supported by two additional bloggers to create two teams of three people each to compete in the cook-off. One team included San Diego designer Brandon Smith, Stacy Garcia, owner of Garcia Cabinetmakers in Huntington Beach, California, and Paul Buchanan, chef and owner of Primal Alchemy Catering in Long Beach, California, who specializes in local, seasonal, and sustainable cuisine.

Their opponents included Rebecca Reynolds, owner of Culinary Kitchen Design in Greenwich, Connecticut, Lori Gilder, interior designer, principal of Interior Makeovers in Beverly Hills, California, and Jennie Cook, local food advocate, blogger, and owner of Plant-Based Parties/Vegan Events in Los Angeles. Leanne developed the cook-off ingredients, focusing on two terrific community builders: chocolate and bacon.

American Standard supplied a working sink and kitchen faucet. The designers were able to talk about their experiences cooking with Capital and washing up with American Standard—a win-win for both brands.

The conversations on Twitter and Facebook groups began to heat up three weeks before the event, ultimately generating more than 3 million views for the participating brands, along with increased engagement and discussions on Facebook. The one-hour cook-off attracted more than 50 spectators to the capital booth. Both brands increased their network of followers and were able to communicate important benefits about their products at the show, as well as via social media. The high visibility at the show helped American Standard catch the attention of *Dwell* magazine editors, resulting in product coverage in the magazine in late 2012. Once upon a time, an idea like the cook-off would have come from the marketing department. Today, great ideas come from collaborating and connecting on social media, where the next good ideas might very well come from your customers.

Planning a Strategy

ow you know that SMM is much more than just having a Facebook page! You must provide customers with real-time interactive assistance across multiple devices—from smartphones to tablets to PCs. In other words, companies need to be where their customers are and be ready to meet their needs immediately. I've shown you how using SMM can dramatically increase your visibility and help you increase sales. You can create a strategy to use this powerful and popular medium to reach buyers.

First, assemble a team because one person in your marketing department can't do it alone. Train everyone in your company to participate in your social media program so they are empowered to successfully use websites to reach target audiences. Get your sales team to participate in your social marketing. Because they interact daily with your customers they need access to all the social media accounts and training to use the accounts effectively. And with the sales and marketing functions becoming more closely aligned, your sales team has a tremendous stake in the success of the companies they represent.

After your team is in place, make sure your website is interactive. Once you get your social media program off the ground, there is nothing worse than directing interested customers to a boring, static website. Make sure yours is engaging enough that they will stay long enough to find the information they need and perhaps even contact you for more information. Then do these 10 things:

- Establish goals for your SMM strategy and write them down.
- Purchase a smartphone, digital camera, and other tools as needed.
- Launch a blog, enlisting a professional or company with a track record of building successful programs.
- Create an editorial calendar.
- Repurpose press releases, e-flyers, and other marketing materials for various online channels.
- Contribute to blogs for your industry.
- Create pages on social networking sites.
- Interact in the social media sphere and build lists of prospects, customers, and influencers. Don't forget to include prominent bloggers.
- Send strategic e-blasts. Establish a schedule for distributing email messages consistently. This

could vary from quarterly to weekly depending on the size of your company and the number of audiences to whom you send email. Use software that allows recipients to opt out and has analytics for you to measure your success and determine how to follow up.

- Track results and update your strategy as needed. Tracking what works and what doesn't allows you to make smarter marketing decisions. You will be able to analyze results and make changes monthly and perhaps even weekly.

Figures 10.1 and 10.2 are sample plans and worksheets for the first and second months of your strategy.

Month One

The size of your program and of your implementation team may warrant spending two months, rather than just one, on setup. In this phase, you will create your strategy, establish your social media policy, and begin to build your social media presence as follows:

- Create your strategy.
- Set realistic, measurable goals.
- Determine keywords.
- Create an editorial calendar.
- Build your online presence.

Company Name			
Project	**Status**	**Assigned**	**Link (if applicable)**
Month, Year			
Strategy	complete		
Goals	complete		
Determine keywords	complete		
Create editorial calendar	In process		
Build blog			
Create Facebook page			
Create Twitter account			
Create ActiveRain account			
Create Trulia account			
Update YouTube channel			
Review/Update Linkedin page			
Create Flickr account			
Create PR.com			
Create Networked Blog account			
Import blog into Facebook page			
Connect blog to Twitter			
Research external sites and blogs			
Netweave—add buttons and links			
Set up website & blog tracking			
Set up Google Alerts™			
Set up other tracking—Twitter, etc.			
Review Google Analytics™ and create baseline			

Figure 10.1 **Sample plan for month one**

Focus on setting up all accounts and interconnecting them during the first month.

Date, Year	Status	Assigned	Link
Complete Tracking Report for previous month			
News Release #1			
Post on PR.com			
Post on PressReleasePoint			
Post on PRLog			
Post on NHDBuzz			
Repurpose for NewHomesSection			
Post on Yahoo Buzz			
Repurpose for Activerain			
Repurpose for Trulia			
Repurpose to Local Niche blog			
Repurpose for Local Industry blog			
News Release #2			
Post on PR.com			
Post on PRWeb			
Post on PRFree			
Post on NHDBuzz			
Bookmark on Delicious			
Repurpose for Activerain			
Repurpose on Trulia			
Repurpose to Local Niche blog			
Repurpose for Local Industry blog			
Blog Posts			
1 - Repurpose News Release #1	Wk 1		
2 - Community Info	Wk 1		
3 - Homebuying Info	Wk 2		
4 - Community Info	Wk 2		
5 - Repurpose News Release #2	Wk 3		
6 - Homebuying Info	Wk 3		
7 - Community Info	Wk 4		
8 - Community Info	Wk 4		
Other Sites			
Linkedin – update personal status to link to a blog post with a shortened URL			
Linkedin – make comments on others announcements, make referrals, seek new connections, make sure employees are listed on corporate profile			
Twitter – develop a schedule of what to tweet in between the 8 tweets from the blog			
Twitter – add relevant followers			
Facebook – develop a schedule of posts for in between the 8 posts from the blog			
Facebook – interact with agents, add relevant Friends and convert them to Fans			
Update Flickr pages - add new photos			
Update Facebook - add new photos			
Train agents on how to tweet, RT, etc.			
Answer Q&As on Trulia			
Join groups on Active Rain			
Comment on other industry blogs			

Figure 10.2 Sample plan for month two

Developing and posting content is the focus of month two.

- ○ Blog
- ○ Social networks
- ○ Online PR sites
- Research external blogs and sites. Find one or two sites to contribute to and enlist guest experts to blog on your site.
- Netweave all sites with buttons, logos, feeds, and applications.
- Track results.
- Set up analytics for the website and blog and create baseline reports.
- Set up Google Alerts.
- Create Twitter searches.
- Consider purchasing a social media monitoring program.

Month Two

As you move into month two and beyond, you'll settle into a routine of pushing your marketing messages out, monitoring the response, and interacting with your online community. Listen, engage, and respond appropriately!

- Disseminate two press releases and post them on PR sites.

- Repurpose press releases to post on other external sites.
- Publish eight blog entries.
  - Create two by repurposing press releases.
  - Discuss overall industry news in two.
  - Focus on community news or company news in the other four.
- Link to the press releases and blog posts from your Facebook page and Twitter account.
- Post at least four messages on external blogs.
- Comment on two blogs.
- Seek new Facebook fans and Twitter connections weekly.
- Post on Facebook.
- Interact on Twitter.
- Post on Google+.
- Add photos and video to Flickr, Pinterest, and YouTube.
- Train sales associates to use Facebook, Linkedin, blogs, and other social media and social networking sites.
- Monitor websites and respond to questions and comments.
- Review progress toward goals and adjust strategy and tactics as necessary.

Larger companies may need to add to these sample plans, whereas smaller ones may wish to scale them back. Once you determine the strategy and staffing that works best for your company, SMM will become part of your marketing routine just as updating pricing or planning for weekend signage is.

SMM will continue to change and evolve. However, your blog will remain the hub of your program. With your own self-hosted WordPress blog, you won't have to rely on the ever-changing social networks to get your message out. Your blog is the component of your program that you own and control. A well-built blog will be one of your website's top referring sites.

Used effectively, SMM is a tremendously powerful marketing tool. Companies can raise their online visibility, improve SEO, increase the number of qualified leads, connect with customers and prospects, and ultimately, sell more products and services. Embracing this medium to reach out to potential buyers is necessary to successfully market and sell today.

As you build your program, please friend, fan, or follow me and let me know how it is going. I'm easy to find: just Google my name or look for me at http://www.mRELEVANCE.com, http://www.CarolMorgan.net, http://Twitter.com/AtlantaPR, or http://www.Facebook.com/CarolMorgan007. I'm on lots of other sites too. If you don't find me where you are, shoot me an old fashioned email and ask me to join you!

Notes

[1] Paul Chaney, *The Digital Handshake: Seven Proven Strategies to Grow Your Business Using Social Media* (Hoboken, NJ: John Wiley & Sons Inc., 2009).

[2] *The Future of Retail Study* (Motorola Solutions Inc., June 2012), http://mediacenter.motorolasolutions.com/Content/Detail.aspx? ReleaseID=14493&NewsAreaID=2&ClientID=1.

[3] comScore Reports $44.3 Billion in Q1 2012 U.S. Retail E-Commerce Spending, May 9, 2012, http://www.comscore.com/ Insights / Press _ Releases / 2012 / 5 / comScore _ Reports _ 44.3 _ Billion_in_Q1_2012_U.S._Retail_E-Commerce_Spending.

[4] *The Future of News* (Pew Research Center's Project for Excellence in Journalism (PEJ) in collaboration with The Economist Group, October 1, 2012), http://www.journalism.org/analysis_report/ future_mobile_news.

[5] Mitch Levinson, managing partner, mRELEVANCE, in personal communication with the author, October 2009 and October 2010.

[6] "The 2012 State of Inbound Marketing" (Hubspot, March 2012), http://blog.hubspot.com/Portals/249/docs/ebooks/the_2012_ state_of_inbound_marketing.pdf.

[7] Free Themes Directory (WordPress.org, accessed March 19, 2011), http://wordpress.org/extend/themes/browse/popular/.

8 "FTC Published Final Guides Governing Endorsements, Testimonials" (*Federal Trade Commission Blog*, October 5, 2009), http://www.ftc.gov/opa/2009/10/endortest.shtm.

9 "Our New Search Index: Caffeine" (*Google Official Blog*, June 8, 2010), http://googleblog.blogspot.com/2010/06/our-new-search-index-caffeine.html.

10 Daniel Tynski, "8 Attributes of Content That Inspire Action" (seomoz Blog, June 19, 2012), http://www.seomoz.org/blog/8-attributes-of-content-that-inspires-action.

11 "S&A Homes Offers E-Incentive for Realtors" (*S&A Homes Blog*, August 23, 2010), http://www.sahomesblog.com/2010/08/sa-homes-offers-e-incentive-for-realtors/.

12 "4 Tips to Improve Your Credit Score" (Chicagoland Real Estate Forum, September 13, 2010), http://www.chicagolandrealestateforum.com/2010/09/13/4-tips-to-improve-your-credit-score/.

13 Chris Parks, "The 6½ Best Reasons Not to Build a Boone Home" (BooneHomes.net, March 19, 2010), http://www.boonehomesblog.com/builder-news/custom-home-builder-boone-homes/.

14 Laura Spencer, "Laundry—the Easy Way" (BooneHomes.net, June 16, 2010), http://www.boonehomesblog.com/builder-news/laundry-the-easy-way/.

15 Douglas Quenqua, "Blogs Falling in an Empty Forest" *The New York Times* (June 5, 2009), http://www.nytimes.com/2009/06/07/fashion/07blogs.html?_r=2.

16 Fair Use (U.S. Copyright Office, accessed January 28, 2011), http://www.copyright.gov/fls/fl102.html.

[17] Duplicate Content (Google Webmaster Tools, accessed October 2, 2010) http://www.google.com/support/webmasters/bin/answer.py?hl=en&answer=66359.

[18] Facebook Key Facts, Facebook Newsroom, accessed February 18, 2013, http://newsroom.fb.com/Key-Facts.

[19] Facebook Timeline Guidelines, https://www.facebook.com/help/?faq=276329115767498

[20] Kunar Patel, "How Your Likes Are Turning Facebook Into the Loyalty Card of the Internet," *Advertising Age* (September 20, 2010), http://adage.com/digital/article?article_id=145982.

[21] Facebook contest policies, http://www.facebook.com/page_guidelines.php.

[22] Twitter, Wikipedia, accessed February 18, 2013, http://en.wikipedia.org/wiki/Twitter.

[23] How to build Twitter lists, https://support.twitter.com/articles/76460-how-to-use-twitter-lists#.

[24] YouTube Statistics, accessed February 18, 2013, http://www.youtube.com/yt/press/statistics.html.

[25] The Infinite Dial 2012, Edison research and Arbitron, May 2012, http://www.edisonresearch.com/wp-content/uploads/2012/04/2012_infinite_dial_companion_report.pdf.

[26] *2012 Social Network Analysis Report*—Demographic—Geographic and Search Data Revealed (Ignite Social Media, July 2012), http://www.ignitesocialmedia.com/social-media-stats/2012-social-network-analysis-report/#Pinterest.

[27] Pinterest Stats (Repinly, November 2012), http://www.repinly.com/stats.aspx.

28 "Pinterest users time on site nearly matches YouTube" (AG Beat, March 3, 2012), http://agbeat.com/real-estate-technology-new-media/pinterest-users-time-on-site-nearly-matches-youtube/.

29 "Online Consumer Pulse Pinterest vs. Facebook: Which Social Sharing Site Wins at Shopping Engagement?" (Bizrate Insights, October 15, 2012), http://bizrateinsights.com/blog/2012/10/15/online-consumer-pulse-pinterest-vs-facebook-which-social-sharing-site-wins-at-shopping-engagement/.

30 "Foursquare Statistics: 30 Million Users, 3 Billion Check-Ins," Stat Spotting, accessed February 16, 2013, http://statspotting.com/foursquare-statistics-20-million-users-2-billion-check-ins/

31 Shannon Manso, sales manager, BHI, in personal communication with the author, October 2009.

32 "The 2010 Mobile Year in Review" (comScore, February 2011), http://www.comscore.com/layout/set/popup/request/Presentations / 2011 / 2010 _ Mobile _ Year _ in _ Review _ PDF _ Request?req=slides&pre=The+2010+Mobile+Year+in+Review.

33 "Mobile Users Ready for Location-Based Text Marketing," (*eMarketer,* July 26, 2010), http://www.emarketer.tv/Article.aspx?R=1007782&AspxAutoDetectCookieSupport=1.

34 Jack Loechner, "Almost as Good as a Sandwich Board" (*Media Post: Online Media Daily,* October 27, 2009), http://www.mediapost.com/publications/?fa=Articles.showArticle&art_aid=116066.

35 *Social Media Survey* (Brunswick, March 11, 2011), http://www.brunswickgroup.com/insights-analysis/surveys.aspx.

36 Giselle Abramovich, "Vast majority of journalists look for news online," www.DMNews.com, (New York: Haymarket Media

Inc., July 26, 2007), http://www.dmnews.com/vast-majority-of-journalists-look-for-news-online/article/97998/.

[37] "National Survey Finds Majority of Journalists Now Depend on Social Media for Story Research" (The George Washington University, January, 21, 2010), http://www.gwu.edu/explore/mediaroom/newsreleases/nationalsurveyfindsmajorityofjournalistsnowdepend onsocialmediaforstoryresearch.

[38] Sharlyn Lauby, "10 Must-Haves for Your Social Media Policy" (Mashable: The Social Media Guide, June 2, 2009), http://mashable.com/2009/06/02/social-media-policy-musts/.

[39] Laurie Burkitt, "Marketers Grapple with Brand-Bashing 'Badvocates'," (*Forbes.com,* October 23, 2009), http://www.forbes.com/2009/10/23/general-motors-american-airlines-cmo-network-badvocates.html?partner=email.

[40] Adam Ostrow, "Social Media Integration Drives Major Clicks for E-mail Marketers" (Mashable, June 21, 2010) http://mashable.com/2010/06/21/social-media-email-marketing-2/.

[41] "New Chart: The Benefits of Sharing E-mail Content with Social Media Sites," (Warren, RI: MarketingSherpa LLC, October 27, 2009), http://www.marketingsherpa.com/article.php?ident=31425.

Glossary

algorithm. A numerical weight Google assigns to each element of linked documents with the purpose of measuring each element's relative importance. The algorithm changes frequently and is generally thought to be based on a mixture of incoming links, the quality of content, and the quality of sites.

analytics. Raw data available from website or blog tracking programs that note the number of unique visitors, hits, *bounce rates,* and other information.

anchor text. Clickable words in a link. Also called a *hyperlink.*

applications. Software programs that perform specific tasks, commonly referred to as apps.

A record. The Internet address record, or IP address of a domain. The A record for the blog http://www.AtlantaRealEstateForum.com is the IP address 204.232.246.163.

baby boomers. The 76 million people born between 1946 and 1964

badvocate. Advocate who uses his or her influence to spread negative information

blog. A web log, a type of website that typically focuses on one subject and displays posts in reverse chronological order.

bot. A software application that can perform an automated task such as scanning the Internet or completing a form

bounce rate. The percentage of website visitors that leave a site without going further than the home page or initial landing page. A bounce can occur when a site visitor clicks on the back button or something on your site that takes them to a different site, such as your Twitter page or a special offer.

call to action. A contact form, banner, or button that prompts a website visitor to click it and continue through the buying cycle.

CAPTCHA. Randomly generated text designed to generate a response to ensure than the respondent is a human being and not an autobot

content management system (CMS). Computer systems used to control and manage data that is accessed and updated by a number of people.

Creative Commons license. A content usage license whereby the owner keeps the copyright but allows others to copy and distribute the work as long as the user credits the originator and conforms to other specific guidelines

crowd sourcing. Soliciting input from an online group of people to get buy-in, ideas or content

custom URLs. Also called vanity URLs, these locators are like a vanity license plate and can include your company name or a keyword phrase.

customer relationship management (CRM). A system or software to track and manage companies' interactions with consumers

cyberstalker. A person who uses the Internet to discover information about another individual, which he or she then uses to cause harm by threats, accusations, or other means.

dateline. The date of your press release and the city and state from which the news originates

direct messaging (DM). A method of messaging another Twitter user, similar to an email message. To DM, add a D and a space before a Twitter user's name to send the tweet directly to that user.

dots per inch (dpi). Pixels per inch. An indicator of image resolution or quality

DSLR camera. Digital single lens reflex camera, a digital camera that combines the parts of a single-lens reflex camera and a digital camera to replace film

e-blast. An email message sent to a large group of people

editorial calendar. A schedule of stories or blog entries created in advance to control and organize content over a period of time.

elevator speech. Your company's succinct brand statement that tells who you are, what you do, and what you stand for.

fans. Same thing as *followers* or friends. People who follow you or your company on various social networking sites.

followers. *See* fans

Four Ps. Product, price, place, and promotion.

friends. See fans

generation X. The 41 million people born between the mid-1960s and the early 1980s. This generation tends not to be brand loyal or receptive to traditional advertising methods.

generation Y. Also called "millennials" or "echo boomers" (children of the baby boom generation), this is the generation that followed generation X. It includes 80 million people born between the 1982 and 1995. They are more socially liberal and are constant communicators who are connected 24/7.

geofencing. Using presence technology to determine when customers are near your place of business

group think. A result that occurs when a group of people striving for conformity reach an incorrect or deviant outcome

hard coding. A website development technique that inputs data directly into the source code of a program instead of formatting through the program itself

hashtag. The pound sign (#) when used as a method for categorizing tweets on Twitter. It simplifies searching specific subjects and tracking trends. Twitter can now be searched without the use of the hash tag, but many people still use the tag to organize content.

hexadecimal code. A number that represents a color displayed online.

hyperlink. A clickable link to another Internet site, often referred to as anchor text.

Hyper Text Markup Language (HTML). A language used to build web pages that includes markup tags and angle brackets. Tags typically are used in pairs to delineate where an element, such as a paragraph or a subheading, should begin and end.

influencer. A person who holds sway over your potential buyers, including a real estate agent, vendor, or friend.

IRL. In real life

JavaScript. A programming language that enhances functionality for creating more dynamic websites

keyword. A word or phrase that directs an Internet user or a search engine to a relevant web page

keyword-optimized title. Using search engine optimized keywords in the titles of blog posts or other media posted online.

Like. A button you can click on Facebook to give positive feedback to a friend about a post

link juice. The quality of a website's link power as determined by its Page Rank and the quality of its backlinks.

list. A Twitter feature you can use to organize tweets

long-tail keywords. Typically product-specific phrases of three to five words. For instance, rather than searching for the word "car," a buyer might search for "1960 restored red Mercedes Benz."

masthead. The title of a website that appears at the top of the page

microblog. A site that allows users to post short messages that are transmitted to others via the Internet. Twitter is a microblog.

netiquette. A contraction of network and etiquette or Internet and etiquette. It is a set of guidelines for how to conduct yourself online.

netweave. To connect online sites and channels to one another

online public relations (PR). Posting press releases with keywords online for visibility and SEO

online sales counselor. An individual responsible for responding to web leads and interacting with potential buyers to set appointments at specific communities with the on-site agents

organic results. Search results that appear because of their relevance to the search term. They are not paid advertisements.

pay-per-click. Internet advertising model in which advertisers pay according to the number of clicks on an ad

permission-based marketing. Marketing to prospective customers who have opted in and consented to receive marketing materials or other information via social networking sites

plug-in. A computer application that serves to extend or interact with a web program or browser

push advertising. Communicating an advertising message to Internet users that they have not requested

quick response (QR) code. A two-dimensional code, similar to a bar code, that takes users to Web-based content, such as a video with product information.

real simple syndication (RSS). An easy way to distribute blog news via email and Internet sites.

referral site. A website that refers traffic to another site. The links may be organic or paid for by the destination site owner.

referral source. *See* referral site

referring URLs. Any website that refers traffic to your website

refuseniks. Members of generation Y who choose not to use social networking sites despite peer pressure

relevance. Online content's pertinence or connection to a given topic.

retweet (RT). Sending a tweet from another user; similar to forwarding an email message.

return on investment (ROI). A measure of profitability versus the amount of money and time invested.

search engine marketing (SEM). Promoting a website to the search engines using both paid ad placements and organic search or SEO

search engine optimization (SEO). Using various tools and techniques to ensure a website appears high in *organic results* for a variety of keywords or phrases. Both on-page (on the website) and off-page (placed on other sites) content can be used to achieve SEO.

search engine results page (SERP). The page that displays when a user types a phrase into a search engine

snark. A person who makes sarcastic comments

sociable icons. Sometimes called "sociable logos," these are the clickable pictures associated with social networking and social bookmarking sites. Including them on e-newsletters and blog posts facilitates sharing.

social bookmarking. A method for storing, organizing, and sharing favorite websites by saving them to sites such as Digg, delicious, and Newsvine.

social media. Tools such as blogs, social networking websites, and social bookmarking.

social media marketing (SMM). The creation and distribution of content and messages on the Internet using social media, including blogs, wikis, forums, photo galleries, video, microblogs; social networking sites like Linkedin, Facebook, and Myspace, and social bookmarking. Anything one does to interact with others online outside the user's website.

social media optimization (SMO). Increasing a website's visibility and traffic using social media and search engines

social media policy. Guidelines for how a company and its employees interact online

social networking. Engaging others in two-way interaction by creating online communities

social sharing. Including social media links as an easy way for participants to share your e-newsletters and blog posts with their friends via their social networks

spammer. A person or organization distributing unsolicited and unwanted bulk email to large groups of people

sticky. A descriptive term for a website that holds the user's attention as demonstrated by the amount of time and the depth of pages they visit on a site

stream. On Twitter, all the tweets you can see on your home page. The stream shows all of your followers' tweets. Depending on how many you follow and how active they are, these can change rapidly.

stuffing. Randomly adding keywords to Internet content to try to improve search results.

tagline. A slogan or memorable phrase that summarizes a product. It is often used to brand a company via marketing and advertising materials.

tag. A keyword used in a blog post or on a social networking site typically used to help search engines find relevant content. Also, a tag is often used to categorize information on blogs and on websites such as Pinterest. Tags do not have to be keywords, although often they are.

teaser. Short punchy copy that entices the reader to read more. Teasers are often used on blogs or with email marketing.

theme. The overall design of a site, including its appearance and functionality.

tracking software. Software that follows where site visitors come from and where they go. It provides data to inform business decisions.

troll. An individual who posts off-topic messages that are usually hurtful, controversial, or inflammatory to users on Twitter, Facebook, blogs, or other social sites.

tweet. A message posted on Twitter

universal resource locator (URL). The address of a file or website

unique selling proposition (USP). The particular attribute of your product or service that distinguishes you from other competing products and services

username. On Twitter, the name under which an individual's or company's tweets will appear, such as @AtlantaPR. The corresponding Twitter URL is http://Twitter.com/AtlantaPR.

web 2.0. The trend on the World Wide Web to network, interact, and collaborate, which has generated social media, social networking, and blogs.

website analytics. Systematic tracking of website visitors to a specific site to determine patterns and preferences to optimize the site

widget. A space on your blog for placing a plug-in or other functionality

Resources

Blog Directories

Blog directories are like online yellow pages. They create incoming links to your blog. There are hundreds of blog directories, both free and paid. Online Marketing Blog (http://www.toprankblog.com/rss-blog-directories/) has a list. Here are a few:

> Best of Web (http://blogs.botw.org/)
> Blog Catalog (http://www.BlogCatalog.com)
> Bloggeries (http://www.bloggeries.com/)
> Technorati (http://www.Technorati.com)

CRM Programs

> Builder 1440 (http://www.builder1440.com)
> BuildTopia (http://www.buildtopia.com)
> Lasso (http://www.lassocrm.com)
> Pivotal (http://www.cdcsoftware.com)
> Sales Simplicity (http://www.salessimplicity.net)
> Salesforce (http://www.salesforce.com)

Free Blog Platforms

These third-party hosts allow you to set up your own blog:

> Blogger (http://www.Blogger.com), Google's free platform
>
> Real Estate Sites Hub (http://www.RealEstateSitesHub.com), hosted by mRELEVANCE, a free blogging platform targeted to the real estate industry
>
> WordPress (http://www.WordPress.com)

Self-Hosted Blog Platforms

By installing blog software from TypePad or WordPress on your own hosting environment with a unique URL, you will create your own site and control its SEO, custom themes, applications, and other features.

> TypePad (http://www.TypePad.com)
>
> WordPress (http://www.WordPress.org)

Builder Blogs

> Top Builder Blogs (http://topbuilderblogs.tumblr.com). This new-homes-focused web-

site provides examples of home builder and other industry blogs.

Email Marketing Programs

Builder Broker News (http://www.builderbrokernews.com)

ConstantContact (http://www.constantcontact.com)

iContact (http://www.icontact.com)

MailChimp (http://www.mailchimp.com)

Facebook

Networked Blogs (http://www.NetworkedBlogs.com). This application allows you to netweave your blog with Facebook.

RSS Graffiti (http://www.rssgraffiti.com/). An application that will post your blog feed to your Facebook wall.

General Social Media Sites

Mashable, the go-to site for social media news and tips: http://www.Mashable.com.

mRELEVANCE regularly posts social media tips
  targeted to home builders and developers:
  http://www.mRELEVANCE.com
My Tech Opinion addresses technology in the
  real estate industry: http://
  www.MyTechOpinion.com
TechCrunch provides profiles and reviews of Internet products and companies: http://
  www.TechCrunch.com
URL Toolbox: 90+ URL Shortening Services. A
  Mashable blog post that features 90 URL-
  shortening services: http://mashable.com/
  2008/01/08/url-shortening-services/

Google Tools

Gmail (https://www.google.com/accounts/)
Google Analytics (http://www.google.com/
  analytics/)
Google Insights for Search (http://
  www.google.com/insights/search/#)
Google Reader (accessed via your gmail account)

Photo Sharing Sites

Most photo sharing sites have free basic memberships. Read the fine print to discover their terms and conditions regarding commercial use.

Flickr (http://www.flickr.com)
Photo Bucket (http://www.photobucket.com)
Picasa (http://picasa.google.com)
Zoomr (http://www.zooomr.com)

Public Relations Sites

http://www.1888pressrelease.com
http://www.24-7pressrelease.com
http://www.atlantadaybook.com
http://www.bignews.biz
http://www.businesswire.com
http://www.clickpress.com
http://www.craigslist.com
http://www.dbusinessnews.com
http://www.epicpr.com
http://www.express-press-release.net
http://www.fastpitchnetworking.com
http://www.free-press-release.com
http://www.free-press-release-center.info
http://www.ideamarketers.com
http://www.i-newswire.com

http://www.information-online.com
http://www.live-pr.com/en
http://www.mediasyndicate.com
http://www.NashvilleDaybook.com
http://www.newsreleaser.com
http://www.nhdbuzz.com
http://www.openpr.com
http://www.pitchengine.com
http://www.pr.com
http://www.pr9.net
http://www.pressbooth.org
http://www.pressexposure.com
http://www.pressmethod.com
http://www.press-network.com
http://www.pressreleasecirculation.com
http://www.pressreleaseforum.com
http://www.pressreleasepoint.com
http://www.prfree.com
http://www.prfriend.com
http://www.prleap.com
http://www.prlog.org
http://www.prnewswire.com
http://www.prunderground.com
http://www.pr-usa.net
http://www.PRWeb.com
http://www.prwindow.com

http://www.przoom.com
http://www.sbwire.com
http://www.theopenpress.com
http://www.usprwire.com
http://www.webnewswire.com

Real Estate-Focused Sites

Ask Carol (http://www.NHDbuzz.com/
AskCarol). This online service allows anyone
in the new homes industry to ask Carol Ruiz
and Carol Morgan questions on social media
and public relations.

New Homes Directory (http://
www.NewHomesDirectory.com). This online
directory lists homes for sale.

NHD Buzz (http://www.NHDbuzz.com). This
website will post new homes industry press
releases free of charge.

Social Bookmarking Sites

Social bookmarking enables users to organize favorite
sites and share them with friends, fans, and followers.
There are literally hundreds of social bookmarking sites.
Some popular ones follow:

Delicious (http://www.delicious.com)
DIGG (http://www.Digg.com)
MarketingLand (http://marketingland.com/)
Mixx (http://www.mixx.com)
Newsvine (http://www.newsvine.com)
Reddit (http://www.reddit.com)
StumbleUpon (http://www.stumbleupon.com)
YahooBuzz (http://www.buzz.yahoo.com)

Social Media Monitoring

Google Alerts (http://www.google.com/alerts). A
free service that allows you to monitor the
latest news on your company, an industry, or
competitors.

Social Media Policies

About.com Blogging and Social Media Policy
Sample (http://humanresources.about.com/
od/policysamplesb/a/blogging_policy.htm).
A page with sample blogging and social media policies.

Social Media Governance (http://
socialmediagovernance.com/policies.php). A
database of social media policies including

those of various public entities and
corporations.

Social Media Policy Musts (http://mashable.com
/2009/06/02/social-media-policy-musts/).
This is a list of 10 items to include in a social
media policy.

Twitter Resources

The following articles contain tips for increasing your
Twitter followers by industry experts Kevin Rose, foun-
der of Digg and TechCrunch, and Chris Brogan:

Brogan, Chris. "Get More Twitter Followers Today." http://www.chrisbrogan.com/get-
more-Twitter-followers-today/.

Rose, Kevin. "10 Ways to Increase Your Twitter
Followers." http://www.techcrunch.com/
2009/01/25/kevin-rose-10-ways-to-
increase-your-Twitter-followers/.

Twitter sorting applications allow users to sort tweets
easily to stay in touch with friends and participate in
chats, track conversations, and monitor brand. Some of
these applications can be integrated with Facebook and
Myspace:

Hoot Suite (http://www.HootSuite.com)

Tweet Deck (http://www.TweetDeck.com)

Twitter Support (http://twitter.zendesk.com/
portal). A "help" website for the popular
social networking site.

Twitter Tools (http://thetwittertools.com). A
website with 900+ Twitter tools and
descriptions.

Video Resources

MetaCafe (http://www.metacafe.com)

Vimeo (http://www.vimeo.com)

YouTube (http://www.youtube.com)

Index